FOURTH EDITION

FORD'S ABC'S OF WINES, BREWS, & SPIRITS

Gene Ford

GENE FORD PUBLICATIONS, INC.
Seattle
and
WINE APPRECIATION GUILD, INC.
San Francisco

FOURTH EDITION

Library of Congress Cataloging-in-Publication Data

The ABC's of Wines, Brews & Spirits

Gene Ford 168 p.

1. Drinking of alcoholic beverages

Published by
Gene Ford Publications, Inc.
in cooperation with
Wine Appreciation Guild, Inc.
155 Connecticut Street
San Francisco, CA 94107
(415) 864-1202

Published in the United States 10 9 8 7 6 5 4 3 2 1

ISBN 0 932664-79-2

Here's to my family . . .
and that stern virtue—
temperance

PREFACE: FOURTH EDITION

Most of the change we think we see in life is due to truths being in and out of favor.
Robert Frost.

The first edition of this book was released in 1978. Its illustrated questions and answers appeared previously in a syndicated newspaper feature which I authored titled "The Wine & Liquor Uncomplicator." I had joined the sales staff of the Christian Brothers Winery in December 1969. Over the next eight years, beginning in 1970, I wrote hundreds of these features as a way of learning my new trade. I'd raise a question and look to the textbooks for the answer.

In drinking matters, the decade of the 1970s was an ebullient, engaging time. The "wine boom" captivated the media and the public. Open bars appeared in hotel lobbies. Journalists touted social drinking in all the major newspapers and magazines. Everyone wanted to know more about ways of matching good drinks with good foods. Prohibition, at long last, seemed safely interred.

But the 1970s also saw the rebirth of a national temperance movement. The second director of the National Institute on Alcohol Abuse and Alcoholism introduced virulently anti-drinking attitudes into federal policy declaring alcohol "the dirtiest drug we have." The Reagan administration originated the Just Say No and "alcohol and other drugs" mandates which egregiously linked all drinking control policies with the drug war. Since then, millions of federal dollars have flowed through state and local channels into programs hostile to any drinking.

Concurrently, international medical research continued to accumulate evidence that responsible drinking has tangible health benefits, particularly in lessening America's most serious premature killer – heart disease. Then, CBS's *60 Minutes* aired two episodes on The French Paradox which shows that wine-imbibing French citizens have less heart disease than us, while engaging in all the untoward culinary habits. What is a confused public to believe? The august *Journal of the American Medical Association* reported this image conflict as a "Physician's conundrum" – that doctors cannot tell their patients "the finding that total mortality is reduced in those who consume one or two drinks a day as compared to teetotalers."

And, so, we end the Twentieth Century as it began. In a dither about drinking. This Fourth Edition comments on these conflicting social policies and once again asserts the simple verity that responsible drinking – the way that over ninety percent of American drinkers drink– has more benefits to society than costs. It's only, as Robert Frost observed, that this "truth" has long been "out of favor."

Gene Ford

Contents

PART ONE: Information Section

PART TWO: Feature Section

PART THREE: Purchasing And Tasting Section

A

Compleat Body

OF

DISTILLING,

Explaining the

MYSTERIES

OF THAT

SCIENCE,

IN

A moſt eaſy and familiar Manner;

Containing an

Exact and accurate Method of making all the COMPOUND CORDIAL-WATERS now in Uſe,

WITH

A particular Account of their ſeveral Virtues.

As alſo a

DIRECTORY

Conſiſting of

All the INSTRUCTIONS neceſſary for learning the *DISTILLER'S ART*; with a Computation of the original Coſt of the ſeveral Ingredients, and the Profits ariſing in Sale.

Adapted no leſs to the Uſe of private Families, than of APOTHECARIES and DISTILLERS

In two Parts.

By G. SMITH, of *Kendall* in *Weſtmorland*.

The SECOND EDITION.

LONDON:

Printed for HENRY LINTOT at the *Croſs Keys* between the *Temple-Gates* in *Fleetſtreet*. MDCCXXXI.

A Point of View

If all be true that I do think,
There are five reasons we should drink.
Good wine, a friend, or being dry:
Or lest we should be by and by:
Or any other reason why.

— Latin Epigram

Oh, God, that men
Should put an enemy in
Their mouths to steal
Away their brains.
That we should, with
Joy, pleasure, revel and
Applause, transform
Ourselves into beasts.

— William Shakespeare

Perhaps nothing in man's rich history has more profoundly affected his well-being than liquor — for good as well as for evil. As a pleasant release from the anxieties of the day, or as a voracious, consuming addiction, liquor is — and most certainly will be — a constant in the lives of men.

It is sufficient for us to recognize and to accept the enormous impact of beverage alcohol upon our society. Nearly two million of our fellow citizens are employed in making, transporting and selling spirits. Retail sales exceed 32 billions of dollars annually.

Federal and local taxes generate over nine and a half billion each year. It is a usurious fact that taxes amount to about three times the manufactured cost of the product!

Yet, America's overall alcoholic consumption has levelled off in recent years. In all forms, we consume each year about 2.7 gallons for every person over 14 years of age. That may seem a lot, but compare it to Portugal's 6.2 gallons; France's 5.9 gallons; or Germany's 3.9 gallons per person. Admittedly, these others are wine imbibing nations! In our pioneer years, we Americans consumed over 7 gallons per person of distilled spirits, so we have moderated considerably.

In terms of abuse, there is a body of professional opinion that cultural ignorance may be a causal factor. A former director of the National Institute of Alcohol Abuse and Alcoholism has stated that society, rather than individuals, may be the greatest cause of alcoholism. He wrote of findings that societies which have alcohol commonly in the diet — those that sip their alcohols slowly and generally with food in relaxed, comfortable surroundings — have a lower incidence of alcoholism.

The urbane commentator Gilbert Chesterton once said that the two things people did not wish to discuss were religion and politics and that these were the only two things worth talking about! Mr. Chesterton should have added alcohol to his list! There is some evidence that we are emerging from the dark ages in the treatment of alcohol consumption. The point of view of this book is that beverage alcohol as a chemical substance is neither good nor evil. Its uses and abuses, however, are profound commentaries on contemporary society.

Temperance and moderation are the companions of knowledge. We will become more moderate in our use of alcohol as we increase our understanding of the workings of the chemical in our system. This book is directed toward that worthy end.

EVERY ABLE BODIED MAN AND WOMAN PLAYED A ROLE IN THE GRAPE HARVEST (The Christian Brothers)

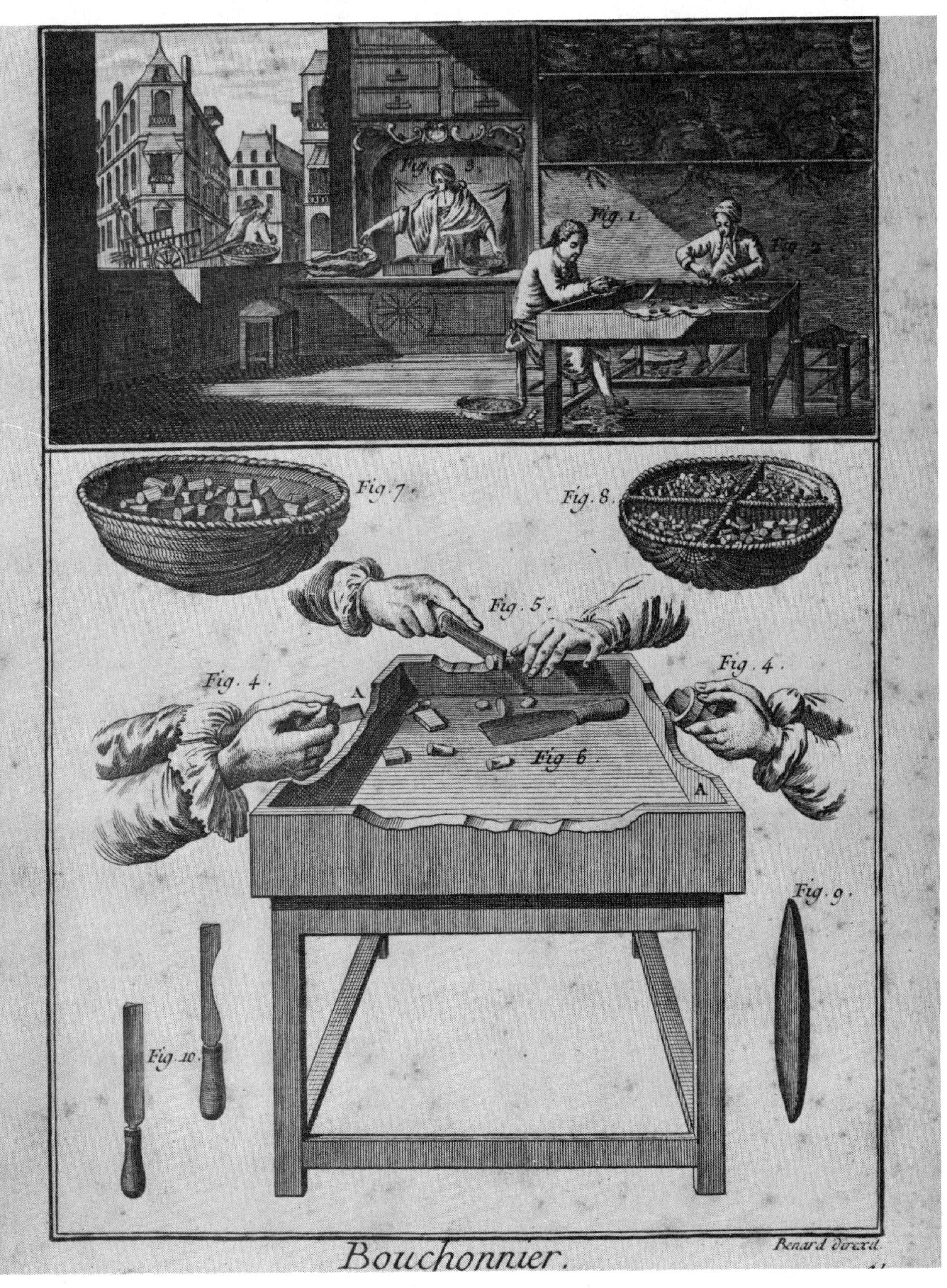

CORK CLOSURES PERMIT THE WONDROUS ALCHEMY OF WINE AGING (The Christian Brothers)

Der Winzer.

Macht euch zum Grab geschickt, eh euch der Tod abpflückt.

Die Zeit legt zu des Winzers Füssen
der Safft-gefüllten Trauben Pracht;
und stolze Schönheit die heut lacht,
wird morgen in die Kelter müssen,
wo Schmertz und Tod die Krafft austreibet,
daß nur die leere Hülse bleibet.

FOR THOUSANDS OF YEARS, MANPOWER CRUSHED THE SKINS FOR FERMENTATION (The Christian Brothers)

How It All Happens

Quickly, bring me a beaker of wine, so that I may wet my mind and say something clever.

—Aristophanes

Wine is constant proof that God loves us and loves to see us happy.

—Benjamin Franklin

Above all, one must clearly understand fermentation and distillation. These two chemical functions, one natural and the other artificially contrived, are the fundamental building blocks of liquor sophistication.

First, visualize a tub of freshly harvested wine grapes. They are luscious, juicy sweet to the taste, and each berry is covered with a wax-like bloom. That sticky substance on the skins traps millions of air-born, microscopic, plant-like organisms. These vital cells are commonly known as yeast.

When the grapes are crushed and the skins broken, the yeast cells enter into the grape juice and begin to break down the natural grape sugars. The thousands of yeast cells rapidly become millions. This process of sugar breakdown is called fermentation. In fermentation, enzymes are secreted by the yeast cells which transform the sugars into almost equal parts of ethyl alcohol and carbon dioxide.

Enzyme is a Greek word meaning "in yeast." Enzymes are non-living materials essential to all biological systems. In fermentation, there are at least twelve distinct enzymatic actions. So, grape fermentation is a quite complex chemical process. After fermentation ceases, the alcohol remains in the must with the spent yeast. The carbon dioxide has floated off into the atmosphere.

Fermentation, then, is a natural process. It can and does occur in the absence of man's guiding hand. If a bird pecks open the skin of a grape, the yeast on the skin can enter the grape and make wine in the vineyard.

But, man is now very much involved in this process. To assure a more stable, longer and more productive fermentation period, most American winemakers wash away the wild yeasts from the skins and impregnate the juice with one or more predictable cultured yeasts.

The process is still natural as this yeast is also one of those found in the field. Since the winemaker harvests his grapes at the precise moment when they achieve the best balance of sugars and acids and he conducts the fermentation in laboratory conditions, his wines are very predictable and quite refined.

The rule of thumb to remember is that the alcohol level in wine is approximately one-half the volume of sugar in the grapes. Wine grapes are picked between 21 and 24 percent in sugar content. The resulting wines average 12 percent alcohol by volume.

The alcohol produced by this process is called ethanol, or ethyl alcohol. There are many other commercial applications for ethanol. It can be utilized as an anti-freeze agent. It is unsurpassed as a rubbing alcohol and commonly sterilizes hospital instruments. It is a familiar component in tinctures and beauty aids. It can be an efficient source of combustion as it burns cleanly with intense heat — as you have undoubtedly noted with the brandy in Cherries Jubilee or Crepes Suzette.

With this process of fermentation creating a ready supply of wine alcohol, let us visualize the next step in the liquor chain called distillation. We place the fermented wine in a huge pot or tank and apply heat. Alcohol vaporizes at about 176 degrees Farenheit, a much lower temperature than the waters and grape solids in the wine. Water boils at 212 degrees Farenheit. The ethanol rises first as a steam and is captured and cooled in a series of copper condensing coils to produce a spirit or liquor, in this case called brandy — or distilled wine.

If we place this concentrated spirit back into another still and repeat the distilling process, we are re-distilling, and the second liquor produced will be purer than the first.

To put it another way, we eliminate more congeners, or grape particles, each time we distill a product.

Now, let's take a look at the proof, or percentage of alcohol in the liquor. Simply, the proof is twice the percentage of alcohol in the bottle. If we distilled the wine at 90 proof, we would produce forty-five percent alcohol by volume. The remaining fifty-five percent would be composed of the other wine fluids and solids. Through re-distilling the same wine to reach 190 proof, we would create a neutral liquor of 95 percent alcohol and only 5 percent of the other wine constituents, mainly water. In all distilling, then, the important decision is the proof at which the liquor is taken from the still.

If, instead of using grapes or fruits, we utilize grains as fermenting materials, we must take an intermediate step called malting. This is accomplished by steeping the grains in warm water until they sprout. This sprouting is called germination. Through germination, another enzymatic action, the grain starches are transformed into sugars. At this point, the material is called malt. It is placed in a mash tank with warm water where the sugars are extracted in what is then called sweet liquor, or a wort. Yeast is added to the wort and fermentation occurs just as it did with the natural fruit sugars in grapes, only now we have a beer. That's what beer is — fermented sugars from malted grains. Many people are happy to stop at this point and enjoy their beers and ales, but the distiller places his beer in a still to produce the stronger liquors.

Hence, brandy is distilled wine and bourbon is distilled beer.

In commercial distilling, the patent or continuous still has the very considerable advantage of handling a continuous flow of wine or beer at the rate of hundreds of gallons per hour. The pot still is limited to a single pot or batch at a time. Consequently, the continuous still is used almost universally in American liquor making, but some pungent pot still spirits are produced for blending purposes.

The next step in the liquor-making chain is aging. Usually the concentrated alcohol is cut or diluted with distilled or demineralized water to a lower proof before storage in fifty gallon oak barrels in huge warehouse. The gentle harmonizing effects of oxidation in the barrels proceed to create a mellow, palatable drink from the fiery young distillate. Sometimes charcoal or wood chip filtering is utilized to accelerate the aging process. During the aging period, the most offensive of the congeners are either eliminated or softened. Most liquors require a minimum of two years in wood, with the top effective limit for most being eight years. However, we still find on the market some brandies and other liquors aged in wood up to 25 years.

Rectifying is next. This function is closely monitored and controlled by the federal government for it is at this point that federal taxes of $10.50 are paid on each proof gallon. Indeed, from the firing up of the still to the sealing of the storebound bottles, agents of the Bureau of Alcohol, Tobacco and Firearms are constant companions of the distiller.

Rectifying can include one or all of the following functions: blending of two different spirits such as a straight bourbon with neutral grain spirits; re-distillation of an already aged spirit to achieve an even lighter, more refined liquor; addition of coloring or flavoring agents, such as the caramel to provide a golden hue to liquor which is almost always naturally white; and, finally, redistillation over flavoring agents such as herbs and botanicals in making gin. It is in rectification that the artisan becomes the artist. The master liquor blender is a supreme judge who can select a blend from literally thousands of tastes and smells in his aging cellars.

From the marriage of twenty to thirty of these separate liquors, he creates the distinctive blends on which success and continuity are based.

Depending upon the liquor, the new blend may have another period of aging before the final step of bottling for sale. At this point, more distilled water is added to reduce the liquor to the final bottle proof. A curious phenomenon occurs in that one gallon of water and one gallon of ethanol combine to making slightly less than two even gallons. The reason is that alcohol molecules are smaller. But never fear, with the government at hand, your every bottle contains the proper amount of alcohol.

And, there you have it. Those are the steps in creating the spiritous products which Raymond Lully so poetically described in the 13th century as . . . "The emanation of divinity destined to revive the energies of modern decrepitude."

THE ART WITHIN EMBELLISHED BY THE ARTISTRY WITHOUT *(German Wine [Information Bureau)*

A Mini Chronology on the Alcohols We Consume

Ancient Times to 500 AD

Paleozoic Era — Honey and grape wines ferment naturally as seas recede and bearing plants develop.

Paleolithic Era — During the Stone Age, nomads settle in permanent shelters, domesticate animals, and cultivate grains and fruits. Beer and wine are common to all ancient diets.

9750 B.C. — The cultivation of seeds, peas, beans and cucumbers is common. Pottery and weaving crafts appear, as does the consumption of alcohol during communal and religious rites.

5500 — Farming in the Tigris-Euphrates river valleys near modern Iran is now common. This is the birthplace of the wine grapes of western civilization.

2800 — The Great Flood: Noah lands the ark at Mount Ararat and makes wines.

1200 to 800 — The Phoenecians of Northern Africa became traders of the Mediterranean, and so further enrich culture and grape development.

600 to 247 (A.D.) — The Roman culture dominates Western civilization. Grapes arrive at Marseille in 600, and from 300 B.C. to 50 A.D. in the French areas of Burgundy, Bordeaux, the Loire Valley, and in Britain and the Rhine and Moselle river valles of Germany.

4 — Jesus Christ is born.

2 — Drinking feasts are common everywhere in Rome where three times as much wine is consumed as in Greece.

410 — The Visigoths sack Rome.

475 — The culturation and development of wine is now controlled by the monasteries of the church.

Medieval Times 500 to 1500 A.D.

550 — St. Patrick brings Christianity to Ireland and probably the distilling techniques he learned in Alexandria.

563 — St. Columba settles in Ionia Island off the coast of Scotland; forms an abbey; and is thought to have distilled the first Scotch whisky.

711 to 1492 — Arabian Moors dominate Spain protect ing vineyards for fruit, but wine abounds despite the prohibitions.

800 — Jaber Ibn Hayyan (Geber), an Arabian alchemist, writes of "al Kohl" in *Liber Investigationes Magisteri.* The report covers the process of raising aqueous vapors: the freeing of liquor in the manner of a common eye cosmetic called "Kohl" which is made from antimony. Also, the Chinese distill spirits from rice wine.

822 — Monks at Weser, Germany, use hops to preserve the flavor brews.

1000 — The Vikings discover America and name it "Vinland" because of the profusion of wild grape vines there. Beer and mead is celebrated in the Anglo-Saxon epic "Beowulf."

1066 — William, Duke of Normandy, conquers England at the Battle of Hastings. French-English wine trade rapidly expands.

1150 — White spirits from sweet fruit is distilled commonly as "alcool blanc." Vodka, or neutral spirits, are first produced from grain in Russia, Poland, and Czechoslovakia.

1172 — King Henry II invades Ireland and discovers a native spirit called "Uisge Beathe" which is made from native grains.

1250 — Apothecaries in Italy commonly produce spirits spiced and sweetened as the earliest of liqueurs.

1290 — Arnald of Villeneuve, a professor of medicine at Montpellier in southern

France, popularizes a medical panacea which he calls "aqua vitae" (the water of life). For the next 400 years, aqua vitae, in numerous forms, comprises a part of medical pharmacopea. "It prolongs life, clears away ill humours, revives the heart, and maintains youth."

1411 The first French distilleries are given licenses in Alsace and Armagnac.

1419 The island of Madeira is settled by the Portuguese and developed for agriculture including grape growing.

1451 German grain spirits called "schnapsteufel" (the devil's drink) are produced, the precurser of modern Schnapps.

1493 On his second expedition, Columbus takes sugar cane from the Canary Islands and plants at St. Croix in the Virgin Islands which sets up the prodigious rum trade.

Early Modern Times 1500 to 1700 AD

1503 Scotland makes peace with England, opening the whiskey trade.

1510 The recipe for Benedictine liqueur is developed, but remains in private hands until 1884

1525 Amaretto liqueur is developed in the town of Sarrona, Italy.

1553 Eau de vie de Cidre, or applejack, is first produced in Normandy, France. It is named Calvados in 1558 in honor of the Spanish Galleon visiting the area.

1561 Beer is first produced for sale in glass bottles in Germany.

1580 Jerez wine is commonly distilled to fortify and preserve Sherry.

1585 Dutch ships carry the first "burnt wine" or brandy from Cognac, France to England and the Lowlands.

1606 The Virginia Company is formed, and early grape growing experiments begin.

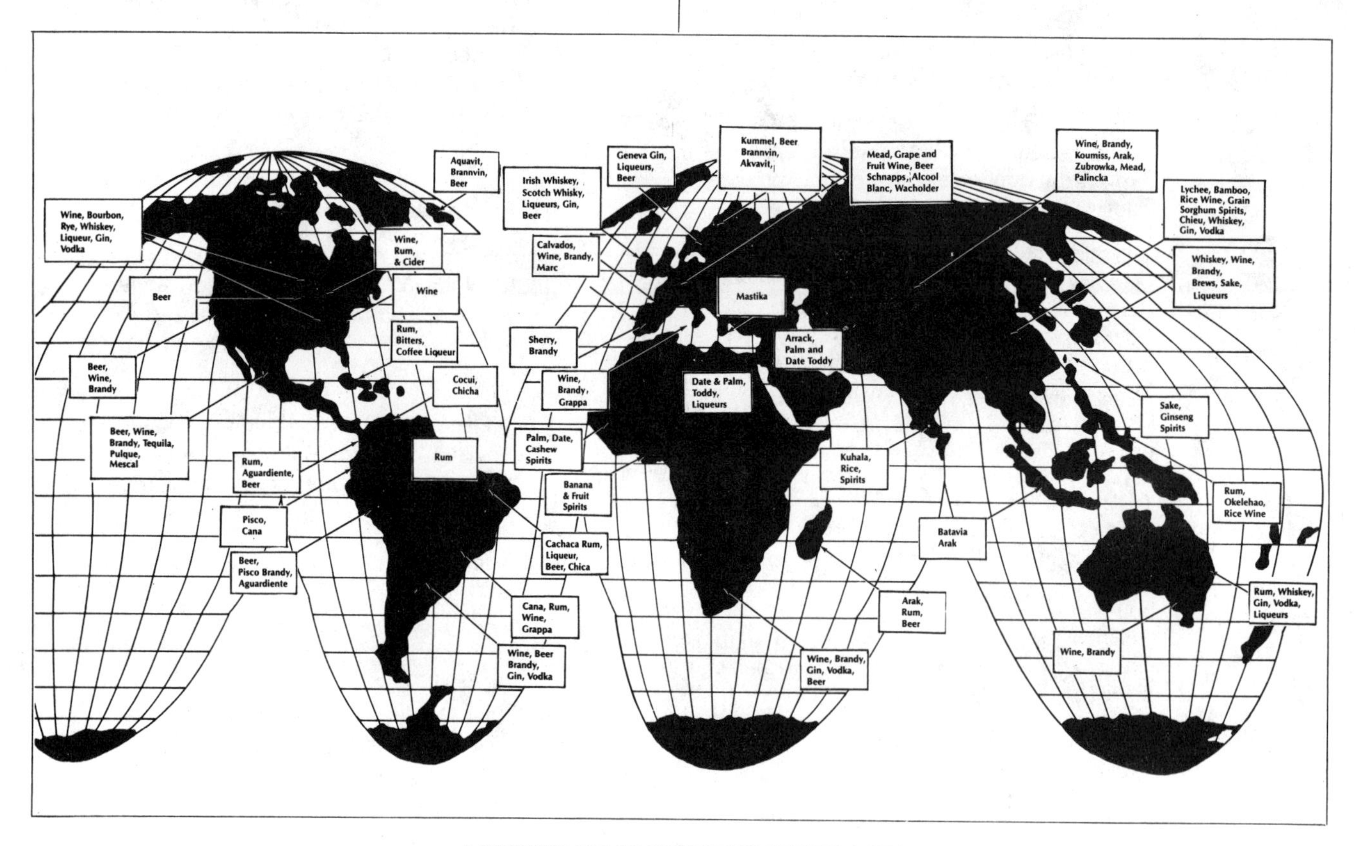

A WORLD OF ALCOHOLIC BEVERAGES

1630 Governor John Winthrop makes the first prohibition move in an attempt to outlaw all liquor in Boston.

1640 Frances Sylvius, at the University of Leyden, Holland, develops a neutral aqua vitae from beer and adds juniper berry as a medicinal diuretic. For western civilization, this well-meaning procedure opened the causeway through which flowed the flood of grain spirits, a ubiquitous source for distillation. Sylvius named his concoction "Jenevre" which was shorted to Gin by the English.

1652 Spirits are made from corn and rye in the first commercial distillery in the United States, operated by William Kieft on Staten Island.

1657 Rum is first commercially produced in Massachusetts from West Indian molasses.

1680 Yeast is first viewed under a microscope by the Dutch scientist Van Leeuwenhoek.

1680 William Penn makes beer commercially in Philadelphia.

1690 Dom Perignon creates champagne in Epernay, France.

1693 William and Mary enact heavy duties to discourage French wine trade, and light duties to encourage Portuguese wine trade.

Late Modern Times 1700 to 1980

1733 Parliament passes the Molasses Act, raising tariffs on non-British molasses to the colonies.

1745 Rum becomes a staple on British navy ships as it is used to prevent scurvy.

1761 George Washington orders a copper still from England and sells spirits commercially the following year.

1769 The art of wine cultivation is brought to California from Mexico by Franciscan priest, Padre Junipero Serra — California's oldest industry is wine making.

1781 The cork is first used as a common stopper, a procedure which allows wine bottle aging.

1789 The Reverend Elijah Craig creates Bourbon from grain whiskey and limestone waters in Kentucky.

1791 The United States government first generates revenue by taxing whiskey and stills.

1808 The first formal Temperance Society in the United States is formed at the First Congregational Church in Saratoga, New York.

1818 Peter Smirnoff opens a vodka distillery in Moscow.

1833 The Supreme Court rules that states can regulate their liquor trade.

1837 Shippers begin to blend neutral corn spirits with rich, malt scotch creating a vast new, international whisky trade.

1843 Captain Sutter produces grape brandy for California gold miners.

1850 A new type of gin is developed in London without sweetener and aptly called London dry gin. Also, Dr. Johann Siegert begins exporting bitters from Angostura, Venezuela.

1852 Madeira wines celebrate their golden age in the United States.

1856 Under a commission of the wine industry, Louis Pasteur isolates yeast as the primary fermenting agent.

1860 Irish distillers begin to blend whiskey with neutral spirits in the manner of the Scotch blenders.

1862 The Bartender's Guide in the U.S. officially labels mixed drinks as cocktails.

1874 The Women's Christian Temperance Union is founded. Also, Prime Minister Gladstone loses his Parliament seat when he attempts to restrict gin consumption.

1876 Beer is first pasteurized for stability.

1880 An estimated eight percent of all Italian workers are involved in the wine industry.

1909 The Cognac area is defined.

1916 Four hundred different individual brands of Irish whiskey are sold in the United States.

1920 On January 16, the 18th Amendment creating Prohibition becomes the law of the land.

1929 The Police Commission of New York City estimates that there are 32,000 speak-easies and twice as many taverns as in pre-prohibition times. They estimate up to a total of 200,000 unlicensed bars in the United States.

1933 On December 5, at 5:32 p.m. the 21st Amendment is passed, ending 13 years 10 months, and 18 days of legal prohibition.

1935 The first beer cans are sold in the United States, and over 700 brewers are involved in the business.

1972 American distillers are permitted to produce light whiskeys reminiscent of the Canadian types.

1978 Over four million cases of Tequila are sold, compared to a total of thirty thousand in 1960.

1980 Sales of Vodka by case to exceed forty million.

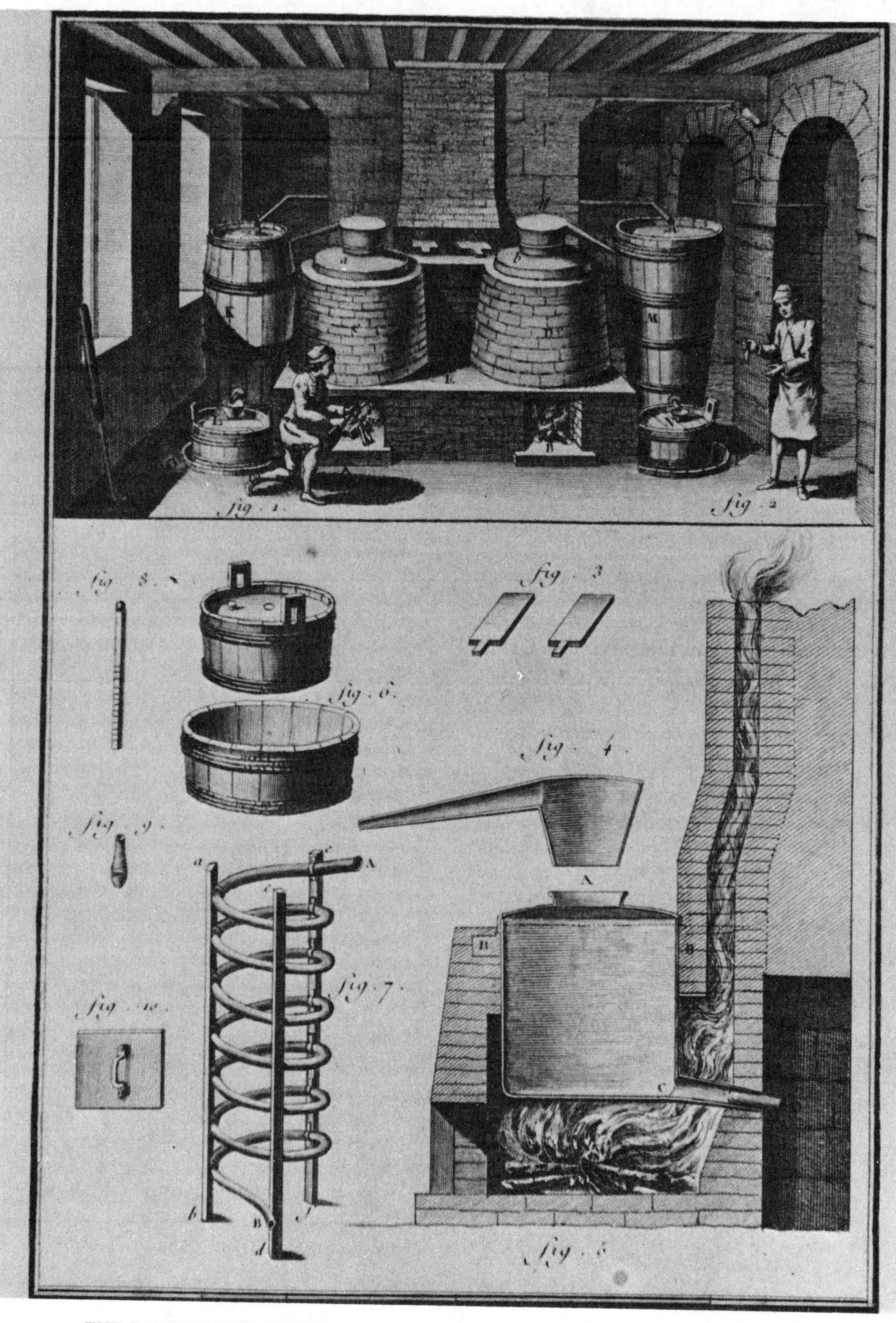

THE SCIENCE AND TECHNOLOGY OF EVERY AGE WAS APPLIED TO DISTILLING
(The Christian Brothers)

Ford's Guide To Choosing The Right Spirit

The age of alcoholic innovation expired with the nineteenth century. Its final accomplishment was the application of the Scottish principle of blending to Kentucky Bourbon and Pennsylvania Rye. By 1900, all the forms of alcohol now known had been discovered, tried, and appraised. The chief concern of the twentieth century has been to appraise the nature of alcohol itself.

—Berton Roueche'

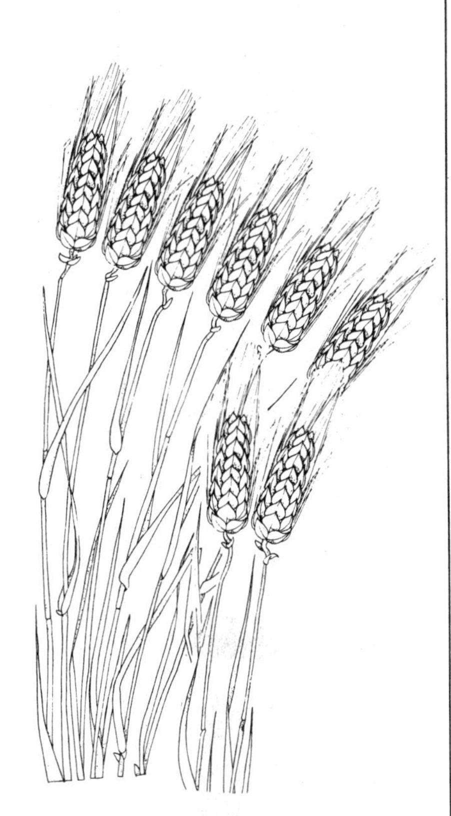

The profusion of brand names and types needn't be all that confusing. Liquors, as other fluids we consume, sort out easily into the strong, forceful or assertive or into the light, mellow and often bland. Source materials and the level of alcohol or proof are the distinquishing elements. The following pages classify the major spirits available in the American market. Generally speaking, the lower the proof the spirit is taken from the still, the stronger the taste of the spirit.

In historical perspective, the wild and woolly variations of quality of spirits in the nineteenth century gave way to two momentuous U.S. government edicts. The first came in 1897 in the Bottled in Bond Act. The second occurred in 1909 when all types of distilled spirits were classified. Throughout the last century, hard liquor was sold in barrels and from hundreds of sources. Much was diluted with raw spirits or water. In times of excess, longer periods of aging occurred in the wood barrels producing mellower products. Hence, the idea of OLD as better took hold, and a few producers began to label their wares such as Old Forrester in 1870 and Old Grand Dad in 1872.

Bottling In Bond encouraged this individuality by assuring the customer of one hundred proof spirits of at least four years of age manufactured by one distiller. The green stamp at that time meant a badge of quality as compared to the uncertainty of open barrel spirits. The classifications in 1909 together with the develpment of new technology for efficient glass bottling assured both quality and identity by brands. The American spirit market bloomed into the advertising bonanza of today. Dozens of companies vie for your attention and dollar. Here are broad outlines for your choice!

CLASS	CHARACTERISTICS
Neutral Spirit	A distillate taken from the still above 190 proof and charcoal treated leaving no taste of original source material. 200 proof is pure alcohol. No character. Bland taste.
Vodka	The one truly neutral spirit as made for the American market. Some import vodkas have light tastes. The perfect base for cocktail mixes that do have tastes.
Whiskey	A bewildering array of choices. Mostly distinguished by character and taste due to distilling below 190 proof and with a particular mash source.
Bourbon Wiskey	Distilled from a minimum of 51% Corn at 160 proof or under and aged in new, charred white oak barrels for a minimum of two years. The oak char, the new barrels and low proof retain many congeners and much character.
Straight Whiskey	Unblended bourbon meeting proof, grain and aging requirements but usually produced at very low proof and aged much longer. Strong and Assertive. If preceded by words such as Wheat, Rye or Corn, the spirit is made from mash with a majority of those grains.
Blended Whiskey	Blends of usually 20% to 35% straight whiskey and grain neutral spirits and/or other agents such as sherry wine. Wide variations available in style and character with consistency the mark of the blender and the label. The objective in blended whiskey is uniform taste from bottle to bottle, year to year.
Tennessee Whiskey	Distillate with bourbon rules that is charcoal filtered immediately after distilling. Great charm and character.
Sour Mash Whiskey	The mash contains about 25% of the residue of a previous mash for added character.
Canadian Whisky	No mistake in spelling. As in Scotland, they drop 'e' in the name. Canadian is a blend with corn the dominant mash together with rye, wheat and barley. With no requirements for new charred cooperage, the spirits are lighter and more mellow. As with Scotch, it is both bottled at home and shipped in bulk for American bottling.

CLASS	CHARACTERISTICS
Irish Whiskey	The only triple distilled spirit in the world, Irish whiskey is prepared from Irish grains and is sold nearly always as a blend. It is supremely light and mellow.
Blended Scotch Whisky	The majority of Scotch has been sold blended since the discovery of the continuous still and grain spirits in 1860's. The base for blending is malt whiskey prepared from pot stills containing characteristic peat smoke and taste. As with American blends individualty of style is prized with each label. Great variation exists but always the smoky finish.
Single Malt Scotch Whisky	Rare but pungently attractive product of the original pot stills with no neutral grain spirits. Great character.
Rum	Distillate produced from by-products of sugar cane with wide variations in style from light Puerto Rican — taken at above 160 proof — to heavy Jamaican — taken often below 140 proof. As a rule of thumb, the white or silver labels are lighter with the gold or amber labels containing heavier spirits.
London Dry Gin	Distillate of nearly neutral spirit re-distilled over bontanicals with juniper berries dominant. The proof of the base distillate contains some flavor and character identifiable in the flavor.
American Dry Gin	The distinction in American gin lies in the use of pure neutral spirits as the base. The redistillation over the botanicals yields no malt or whiskey character but a stronger juniper flavor.
Dutch Gin	Also called Hollands or Scheidam, Dutch Gin retains easily recognizable malt flavoring from the base whiskey. Like the single malt Scotch, Dutch Gin is strong and assertive.
Tequila	Tequila is a low proof, pot stilled distillate from the mash of the heart of the agave plant. Of great individuality and character, some Tequila is aged and in gold labeled bottles. Most is unaged and of light character.
Brandy	Brandy is the distillate of wine or the fermented mash of any fruit. If any fruit other than grape is used, the bottle displays that fruit name. Brandies are made throughout the world in a bewildering array of styles.
Cognac	The popular import brandy derives from a very limited area in Southern France and is produced by double distilling in pot stills and taken at very low proof. Ninety percent is sold at the Three Star level at an average of four years in aging. Cognacs rank among the most pungent and powerful of spirits.
Armagnac	A product of Southern France, Armagnac is double distilled in combination pot-continuous stills, aged in local wood and emerges a slightly harder, cleaner spirit than cognac.
American Brandy	Much greater proportions of continuous still distillage are utilized in producing the lighter, often sweeter American style brandy. For this reason, it is often used as a cocktail base as well as a sipping drink.

THE NEED FOR TIGHT AND DURABLE BARRELS MADE THE COOPER A MASTER (The Christian Brothers)

Ford's Basic Definition List

Drink! For you know not whence you came, nor why.
Drink! For you know not why you go, no where!

—**Omar Khayyam**

Wine is the most healthful and hygienic of all beverages.

—**Louis Pasteur**

ALCOHOL The alcohol to remember is ethyl alcohol, also known as ethanol, a by-product of the fermentation of sugars. A number of lesser alcohols also are created in fermentation in minute quantities, but *ethyl* is the beverage alcohol.

FERMENTATION Fermentation is a form of combustion which realigns each molecule of sugar (carbon, hydrogen and oxygen) creating from each, two new molecules each of ethyl alcohol and carbon dioxide. This is the natural process discovered by ancient man by which fruit becomes wine and germinated grain becomes beer. The process is caused by yeasts which operate under the surface of the grape juice without benefit of air — hence the fermentation is anaerobic.

A STILL A still is a container or device used to vaporize and to capture alcoholic spirits.

A POT STILL The pot still is the oldest, simplest mechanism used in distilling. It is akin to a pot on a stove with an inverted funnel used to catch the alcoholic vapors and a cooling chamber so that the steam can return to a fluid. The pot still cooks one batch of wine or beer at a time. When fully distilled a new batch is placed in the pot.

PATENT OR CONTINUOUS STILL Invented in 1825 by an Irishman with the unlikely name of *Coffey,* a continuous still is simply an ingenious series of pot stills stacked one upon the other, allowing the capturing of vapors or spirits at various levels or proofs. The considerable advantage is that it can handle a continuous supply of wine or beer all day long — hundreds of gallons an hour. This tremendous efficiency factor is the reason that the majority of the world's liquors are made in continuous stills.

MALT OR MALTED GRAIN While the sugars in wine ferment naturally, grain is composed of starch which will not ferment. Hence, malting or the germinating of barley, corn or rye grain is a necessary first step before fermentation. The grain is placed in a bath of warm water. When the grain sprouts, the starch saccharifies, or changes to sugar. This is called malting. The malted grain is then ground and mixed with water and yeast for fermentation.

CONGENER Understand the congener and you will identify the tastes and the character of various liquors. Congeners are elements passed over from the original wine or beer, such as mineral salts, aldehydes, acetic acid, esters and fusel oils or new compounds created in fermentation and distillation. In sum, congeners provide the recognizable spirit tastes and aromas. In heavy concentration, they are often unpleasant, even repulsive. In balance, they delight the senses. Esters are combinations of acids, alcohols and oxygen which create the distinctive fruity aromas as well as the bouqet in aged wines.

FUSEL OILS These congeners are pungent, even nauseous, higher alcohols often called heads or foreshots since they vaporize first in a still at lower heat levels. They precede the true ethyl alcohol vapors which are called middle liquors in distillation.

ALDEHYDES These congeners are volatile fluids created by the oxidation of alcohols and they pass over last in the distillation process at the highest temperatures. Hence, they are termed tails of feints. As with esters, they are important to the bouquet or smell of the liquor.

OXIDATION Oxidation is the chemical process by which wine and all spirits eventually decompose. Think of an apple turning brown when exposed to the air and you visualize oxidation. It is therefore, the fatal enemy of wine, or any other fruit for that matter. By contrast, it is the gentle harmonizer, the mellowing agent for the harsh new liquors. They mellow by oxidation as they rest year after year in the aging barrels. Finally, within our own bodies, ethyl alcohol is oxidized freeing the calories as energy.

PROOF Though the British still use the exact odd percentages, in America, proof is registered as exactly twice the percent of ethyl alcohol in the bottle. A shot of 100 proof vodka is composed of fifty percent ethyl alcohol and fifty percent distilled water. An eighty proof brandy has forty percent ethyl alcohol in the bottle.

PROOF OFF THE STILL The liquors taken directly from the still before being cut or diluted with distilled or demineralized water also are measured in proof. Again, the proof is twice the actual amount of ethyl alcohol in the fluid. The remaining fluid, of course, is constituted of the wine or beer being distilled. An absolutely pure spirit would be all ethyl alcohol without a single trace of wine or beer. So, the proof from the still tells you the percentage of alcohol in the spirit. A liquor taken from the still at 130 proof is constituted of sixty-five percent ethanol and thirty-five percent of the wine or beer from which it was distilled. It has a very high congener count. Obviously, an absolutely pure spirit would be taken from the still at 200 proof. It would be one hundred percent ethanol and nothing else. Thus — a neutral spirit.

NEUTRAL SPIRIT Neutral (formerly called cologne) spirits are those taken from the still at such a high proof that they are colorless and nearly odorless, utterly lacking in congeneric character.

BLENDING This is simply the marrying of two or more liquors or other palatable substances. Consistency is the primary aim of the blender in order that your favorite scotch or cabernet wine tastes the same each time you purchase it.

IN BOND Literally, in bond signifies federal control over the liquor. When referring to whiskey, bottled-in-bond means the product is a straight whiskey, at least four years old, which had been bottled at 100 proof. That's really all it means. It may be superb or quite common whiskey, as the designation has no relation to the quality.

DRY Our final essential term is dry, and it is perhaps the most confusing since it has a number of meanings in alcoholic beverages. As example, dry means a lack of sugar to the winemaker. A medium-sweet wine has a definite sweet overtone. By contrast, a dry gin is one made without a trace of the grain congeners. Dry gin is distilled a second time with herbs and a neutral spirit. Even more confusing, a dry martini is that same dry gin served with but a hint of dry vermouth which itself has some sugar in it. Confused? Oh, well, keep in mind that most often dryness is the absence of sugar in wine.

These are the essential working definitions. They are used repeatedly in the features which follow.

TRADITIONAL EUROPEAN METHODS BECAME COMMON IN EARLY CALIFORNIA DAYS (The Christian Brothers)

A Panorama of Alcoholic Beverages

Aguardiente: rum spirit (Central America)
Aquardiente de uva: spirit of grapes (Spanish)
Akvavit: vodka (Danish)
Alcoholado: cow with black eye markings (Spanish)
Alcool blanc: white fruit spirit (French)
Ale: light top fermented brew (English)
Al Kohl: alcohol or distilled antimony powder (Arabic)
Aperitif: herbed & often sweetened wine (Universal)
Aqua ardens: ardent or spirited water (Latin)
Aqua composita: whiskey punch (Gaelic)
Aqua de vite: water of life or spirits (Italian)
Aqua vini: water of wine (Italian)
Aquavit: flavored vodka (Swedish)
Aqua vgtae: water of life or spirits (Latin)
Arack, arrack: grape, palm, & date spirit (Syrian)
Armagnac: Gascon brandy (French)

Bagaciero: pomace brandy (Portuguese)
Bal: honey wine (Russian)
Barrack palinka: apricot brandy (Hungarian)
Beer: fermented grain (English)
Bitters: liqueur with bittering agent (English)
Bourbon: grain spirit (American)
Bouza: beer (Turkish)
Brandewiin: burnt wine or brandy (Dutch)
Brandy: distilled grape wine (Universal)

Calvados: apple brandy spirit (French)
Canadian: grain whisky (Canadian)
Champagne: white sparkling wine (French)
Champenskoe: white sparkling wine (Russian)
Chica: maize beer (South American)
Chiew: any alcohol (Chinese)
Clairin: single distillation rum (Haitian)
Cocui: cactus spirit (Venezuelan)
Cognac: southern French brandy (French)
Compound: mixture of agents and spirits (Universal)
Congeners: taste and flavor elements in spirits (Universal)
Continuous still: continuously operating still (Universal)

Cordial: United States made liqueur (American)
Corn Whiskey: bourbon made with 75% corn (American)

Courmi: early ale (Gaelic)
Creme: extra sweet liqueur (Universal)

Demarara: heaviest flavored rum (Guyanan)
Dessert wine: alcohol added sweet wine (Universal)
Digestif: liqueur (French)
Distill: to separate alcohol spirits by heat (Universal)
Distillare: to drip down (Latin)

Eau-de-vie: water of lie — spirits (French)
Eiswein: wine from frozen grapes (German)

Ferment: breakdown of sugars by yeast (Universal)
Firewater: spirituous liquor (American)
Fraise: strawberry brandy (French)
Framboise: raspberry brandy (French)
Frucht aromalikors: unflavored fruit brandies (German)
Frucht softlikors: flavored fruit brandies (German)

Geneva: gin spirits (English)
Grain Spirits: alcohol made from grain base (Universal)
Grappa: pomace brandy (Italian)
Grog: early name for Carribean rum (English)

Himbeergiest: raspberry brandy (German)
Hollands gin: malt flavored gin (Dutch)
Honiglikor: honey spirit (German)
Hydromel: honey wine (Northern Europe)

Irish whiskey: triple distilled grain spirit (Irish)

Jamaican rum: medium heavy bodied rum (Jamaican)
Jenever gin: gin spirits (Dutch)

Khometz: vinegar (Biblical)
Kirsch: cherry brandy (Alsatian, German, Swiss)
Kornbrantwein: grain spirits (German)
Kosher wine: wine made under religious rules (Jewish)

Koumiss: wine made from fermented mare's milk (Russian)
Kuhala: barley based spirit (Sir Lanka)

Lager: aged, bottom fermented beer (Universal)
Liqueur: sugared and flavored spirit (Universal)
London Dry gin: unsweetened gin (English, American)

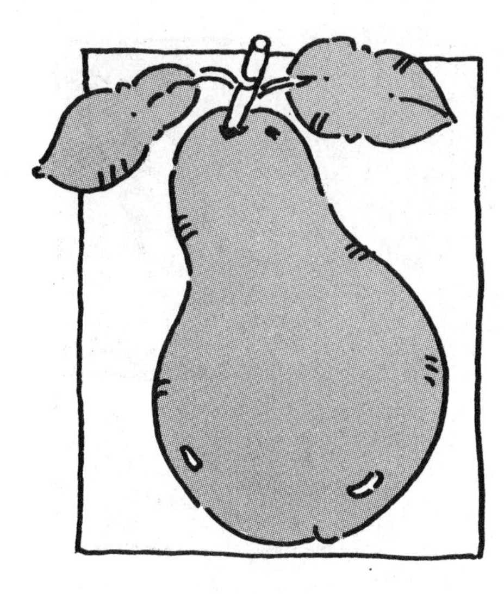
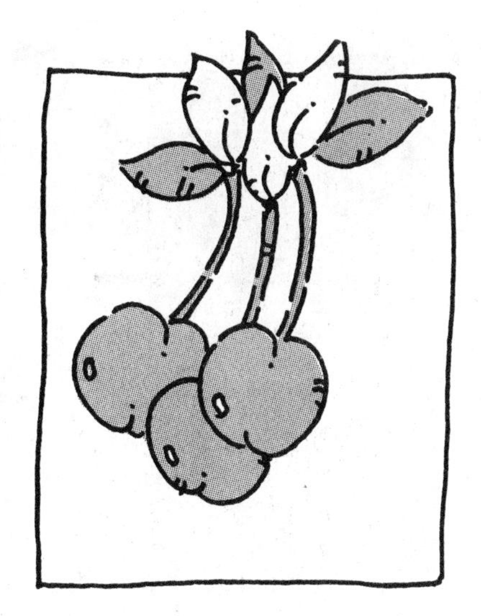

From a World of Fruits and Grains

Madeira: dessert wines from Madeira Island (Portuguese)
Malt whisky: single batch, pot distilled spirit (Scotch)
Marc: pomace brandy (French)
Marsala: dessert wines from Island of Sicily (Italian)
Mash: grain or fruit ready for fermentation (Universal)
Mastika: resin treated brandy (Greek)
Mead: honey wine (Northern Europe)
Mescal: dumpling cactus spirit (Mexican)
Meseg: flavored wine (Biblical)
Moonshine: illicit spirits (American, Irish, Scotch)
Mousseux: sparkling wine (French)
Moutwijn: neutral grain spirits (Dutch)

Nastoika: flavored vodka (Russian)

Okiwata: water of life — spirits (Polish)
Old Tom gin: slightly sweet gin (British)

Percolation: spirit flavoring by seeping (Universal)
Perry: pear based wine (American)
Petillant: partially sparkling wine (French)
Piment: medieval flavored wine (French)
Pisco: grape brandy (Chilean, Peruvian, Bolivian)
Poire William: Williams pear brandy (French)
Pomace: skins, seeds, and pips after winemaking (Universal)
Pop wine: flavored and carbonated wines (American)
Poteen: illicit spirits and the pot they are made in (Irish)
Pot Still: single kettle batch distilling (Universal)
Proof: measure of alcohol content (Universal)

Quetsch: plum brandy (Alsatian, Swiss, Balkan)

Raki: potato, plum, rice, molasses, fruit brandy (Balkan)
Rhum: rum (French)
Roggen: rye grain spirits (German)
Ron: rum (Central American and West Indian)
Rum: sugar cane spirit (English, American)
Rye: whiskey from rye grain (American)

Sacramental wine: wine under religious rules (American)
Sake: rice brew (Asian)
Sauker: liquor (Arabic)
Schaumwein: sparkling wine (German)
Scheidam: malty gin from Holland (Dutch)
Schnapsteufel: brandy devil — alcohol (German)
Scotch: barley and grain whiskies (Scotch)
Sekhor: strong drink (Biblical)
Sekt: sparking wine (German)
Sikera: intoxicating liquor (Biblical)
Slivovitz: plum brandy (Rumanian)
Soma: wine (Biblical)
Sparkling: effervescent wines (Universal)
Spirit Menstrum: water & liquor for steeping base (Universal)
Spirituous vini: wine spirit (Latin)
Spumante: effervescent wines (Italian)
Steinhager: gin spirit (German)

Table wines: still wines (Universal)
Tequila: maguey cactus spirits (Mexican)
Tresterbrantwein: pomace brandy (German)

Uisge Beathe: water of life spirits (Gaelic)

Vermouth: herbed, sweetened high alcohol wine (Universal)
Vinum Ardens: ardent wine (Latin)
Voda: water or white spirits (Russian)
Vodka: pure spirits (American)
Vodnyi vinnyi: grape spirits or brandy (Russian)

Wacholder: corn spirit gin (German)
Weingeist: wine spirit or brandy (German)
Whisky: grain spirits (Scottish)
Whiskey: grain spirits (Irish, Canadian, American)
Wine: fermented fruit (Universal)
Woda: water or white spirits (Polish)

Yayin: wine (Biblical)

Zubrovka: flavored vodka (Polish)

AFTER YEARS OF PATIENT AGING THE SPIRIT IS REDUCED TO MARKET PROOF *(Renfield Importers)*

The Proof of Things

To maintain perspective in beverage alcohol consumption, remember that the proof is exactly twice the volume of alcohol in the drink. In the United States we measure proof spirit as exactly twice the alcohol content by volume at a temperature of 60° F. *However, beer is measured by the weight of alcohol in the fluid and wine is recorded in the exact amount of alcohol by volume.*

Here is a comparison of these three measurements:

BEVERAGE	HOW MEASURED	RANGE OF ALCOHOL	AVERAGE SERVING	APPROX. AMT. OF ALCOHOL
RUM	PROOF	80-151 PROOF	ONE OUNCE per 151 PROOF	¾ OUNCE
BOURBON	PROOF	80-100 PROOF	ONE OUNCE PER 100 PROOF	½ OUNCE
BRANDY	PROOF	80 PROOF	ONE OUNCE PER 80 PROOF	4/10 OUNCE
LIQUEUR	PROOF	54-100 PROOF	ONE OUNCE PER 60 PROOF	3/10 OUNCE
BEER	WEIGHT	3-5.4%	ELEVEN OUNCE CAN	4/10 OUNCE
DESSERT WINE	VOLUME	18-20%	THREE OUNCES	6/10 OUNCE
TABLE WINE	VOLUME	12-14%	FIVE OUNCES	6/10 OUNCE

Calories . . .

	Ounce	Approx. Calories
Glass of Milk	8	160
Dry Martini	2	160
Liqueur or Cordial	2	200
Glass of Beer	12	150
Glass of Dry Wine	4	96
Glass of Dry Sherry	3	99
Glass of Cream Sherry	3	120
Glass of Champagne	3	75
Daquiri	2	150
Shot of Bourbon	1¼	120

OAK WOOD AND TIME COMBINE TO MAKE THE GREAT WINES AND GREAT SPIRITS (National Distillers)

Wine and Sugar Levels

Classification	Sugar Range By Volume	Wine Types
Dry Wines	Zero to 1%	Pinot Noir, Cabernet, Sauvignon, Chablis, Burgundy, Claret, Pinot Chardonnay
Off-Dry	1% to 3%	Chenin Blanc, Rhines, Off-dry Chablis, Liebfraumilch, Extra Dry Champagne, Dry and Cocktail Sherries, Rose' Wines
Medium Sweet Wines	3% to 5%	Golden Sherry, Sauterne, Champagne Rosé, Rose' Wines, Lambrusco
Sweet Wines	7% to 13%	Cream Sherry, Ports, Berry and Fruit Wines, Cold Duck

Cordials and Liqueurs by Taste

MINT
Creme de Menthe——Universal
Peppermint Schnapps——German
Vandermint——Dutch
FRUIT
Sloe Gin——Tart Plum
Framboise (fram-BWAZ)——raspberries
Fraise (FREZ)——strawberries
Cassis (ka-SEECE)——currant
Creme de Banana——bananas
Southern Comfort——peach
TEA
Suntory green Tea——Japanese
VANILLA
Parfait Amour——French
HERB
Ng Ka Pay——Chinese
Chartreuse (shar-TRUSE)——French
Benedictine——French
B&B——French

ORANGE
Cointreau (kwan-TRO)——French
Curacao (cure-a-SOW)——West Indian
Sabra——Israeli
Triple Sec——West Indian
Amer Picon (PEE-kon)——French
CITRUS
Strega——Italian
COFFEE
Kahlua——Mexican
Tia Maria——Jamaican
Creme de Mocha
HONEY
Drambuie (dram-BOO-ee)——Scottish
Irish Mist——Irish
NUTTY
Amaretto——Italian
Creme de Noyaux (know-YO)——French
Persico——English

CHERRY
Cherry Heering——Danish
Kirsch——French
Kirschwasser——German
Wishniak——Polish
CHOCOLATE
Chocolate Marmot——Swiss
Cremè de Cacao——Universal
Creme de Chocolate——South African
Afri-Koko——Sierra Leonese
Vandermint——Dutch
ANISE/LICORICE
Anisette——Universal
Pastis——French
Ouzo——Greek
Mastic——Greek
Sambuca——Italian
Galliano——Italian
CARAWAY
Kummel (KIM-el)——German
Aquavit——Scandinavian

The Rebirth of Prohibition Policies

Prohibition's an awful flop.
We like it.
It can't stop what it's mean to stop.
We like it.
It's left a trail of graft and slime, it don't prohibit worth a dime.
It's filled our land with vice and crime.
Nevertheless, we're for it.

Franklin P. Adams

No one with an ounce of common sense denies the need for drinking control policies. There are two classic approaches to the control of drinking. One works and the other doesn't.

The only successful control system through history is cultural integration which utilizes family and peer pressures to lessen the tendencies to abuse. The second approach depends upon punishments and prohibitions of one sort or another. Our national prohibition failed because of overbearing government intrusion into moral choices. Citizens simply ignored the overly repressive laws.

But repeal in the 1930s did not usher in a new era of cultural integration. Indeed, for many states, the Twenty-First Amendment simply shifted distribution and retailing from criminal elements to legal enterprises. Rum was still "demonized" by elaborate sets of Blue Laws that, to varying degrees, maintained social and political disdain of any and all drinking.

Over the years, these official sanctions were relaxed, state-by-state, and a more open, accomodating atmosphere prevailed. However, in the mid-1970s, as a reaction to this thawing of official policy, the nascent dry movement reappeared with an entirely new and much more creative agenda called the control of availability. In brief, it holds that cutting down all drinking will cut down abusive drinking. On that tenet rests the goal of Health and Human Services in their goal book *Healthy People 2000* of reducing all drinking twenty-five percent by the year 2000. On this base, the government has devised all kinds of demonizing tactics like the adjacent imaging of beer with a hypodermic needle, the use of cops in the classroom to confuse use with abuse and the linkage of drinking with street drugs.

HEALTHY PEOPLE 2000
National Health Promotion and Disease Prevention Objectives

But reason is once again beginning to prevail. Health and Human Services recently joined with the Department of Agriculture in the most recent *Dietary Guidelines* stating that responsible drinking can reduce the incidence of heart attacks and other diseases. National ambivalence about drinking will remain until we drop the insidious "alcohol and other drugs" programs and establish a positive cultural identity for responsible drinking in which a new standard of moderation prevails.

WINES

Wine puts life into a man,
If he drinks it in moderation.
What is life to a man deprived of wine?
Was it not created to warm men's hearts?
Wine brings gaiety and high spirits,
If a man knows when to drink,
And when to stop;
But wine in excess makes for bitter feelings
And leads to offence and retaliation.

Ecclesiasticus 31:27-29

PART TWO: Feature Section

SOCIAL COMMUNION AND GOOD CHEER ARE THE LEGACIES OF A FINE HARVEST (German Wine and Information Bureau)

Fermentation — A Gift In Nature

Who loves not women, wine, and song;
Remains a fool his whole life long.

—Johann Voss

In wine there is truth.

— Pliny

A search of the artifacts and the written literature of all societies, from the most remote of stone-age tribes down through modern cultures, will reveal at least one constant ambivalence — the glowing praise as well as the grudging recognition of the dangers inherent in the consumption of various fermented beverages.

Potable alcohol has been a constant in all societies since it lies in nature as easily accessible as the foodstuffs from which it is made. Anything that will rot can also ferment into some form of alcohol. The one which derives

HAND RIDDLING OF FINE CHAMPAGNE REPLACED BY HUGE TILTING MACHINES
(Piper Heidsick/Sonoma Vineyards)

from the metabolyzing of carbohydrates is called ethanol or ethyl alcohol. It is potable, or drinkable, in moderate amounts.

The root of the word fermentation comes from the Latin and means to boil or bubble. That root also has given us the word *fever*. No wonder, since fermentation is a *feverish* undertaking. All kinds of other ferments occur and are used by man such as in the making of tofu, soy sauce, beef jerky and pickles. Fermentation is also related to the wondrous family of commercial ferments and molds that produce medicines, acids, and food additives.

Fermentation is also a natural process, part of the never ending ecological cycle of birth and death in nature. Therefore, there was wine before man, or at least the *homo sapiens* of our day. If a bird pecks open the skin of a grape, air borne yeast cells will transform the grape sugars into wine right there in the open field.

At a very, very early time, man became a partner in this process. To assure a more stable and certain supply, early man became a vintner. Through the thousands of intervening years, observation and deduction led to a modern science called enology — that of transforming natural grape sugars into wines. Whether accomplished with great deliberation in the highly sophisticated modern winery, or quite casually by a home winemaker, the fundamentals are identical.

A Wedding of Nature and Art

Grapes are harvested at an ideal balance of natural grape sugars and fruit acids. These critical elements predict the future tastiness of the fermented wines. Since grapes produce lots of sugar, and are mineral and vitamin rich, they can more easily support the yeast activity than most other fruits. Therefore, *grape* wines have always dominated as compared to apple or peach wines which often need added minerals and sugars to fully ferment.

A rule of thumb to remember is that the alcohol produced from grapes amounts to approximately one half of the original grape sugar. Hence grapes of twenty four percent produce twelve percent alcohol. Cold climate fruit with low sugar levels often need the addition of more sugar in the fermenting tank to produce an alcohol balanced and tasteful wine.

Now, visualize a tub of freshly harvested wine grapes. They are luscious, juicy, sweet to the taste, and each berry is covered with a familiar wax-like bloom. That sticky substance on the skins traps literally millions of the air-borne, microscopic, plant-like organisms known commonly as yeasts. When the grape skins are broken in crushing, these yeasts enter into the sugar rich grape juice and begin to catalyze or break apart those sugar cells. The yeast cells secrete enzymes which transform the sugars into nearly equal parts of ethyl alcohol and carbon dioxide. This breakdown is called fermentation.

Enzymes are non-living, complex proteins composed of a number of amino acids which are essential to all biological systems. In the fermentation of grape sugars, there are at least twelve distinct enzymatic actions which occur in a wildly orchestrated frenzy. So, grape fermentation is a natural, but a quite complex chemical process. Following this several week period of violent activity, there has been created two observable by-products and many others not quite so evident. The first can be tasted. Ethyl alcohol. The second can be observed during the process. Carbon dioxide bubbles off the top of the tank. Other unseen new products which effect taste and smell are glycerine, acids, esters and aldehydes.

Ford's Easy Outline For Still Wine Fermentation

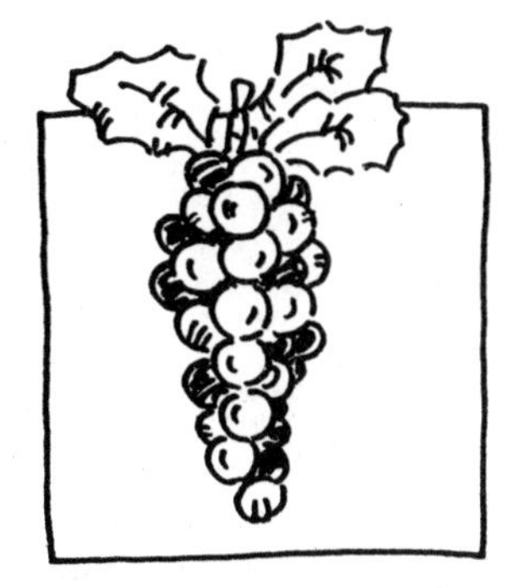

1. Fresh ripe grapes and most other fruits produce naturally fermentable fructose and glucose. These sugars ferment easily in aqueous, anaerobic atmosphere natural to the grape. Most other fruits must have water added to create a fermentable mash.

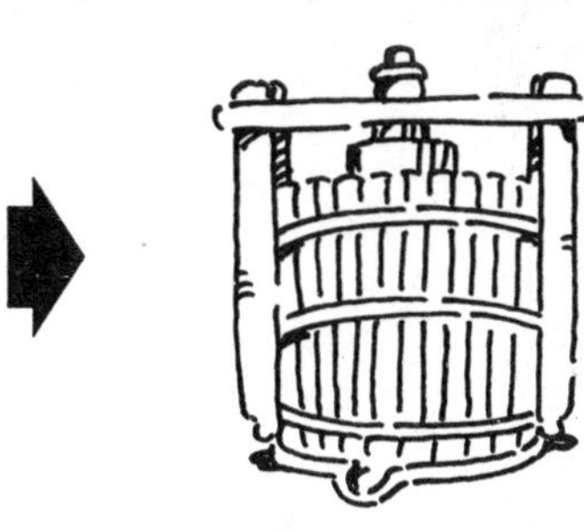

2. Grape skins are broken and the sugary juice is expelled, usually by some form of mechanical press.

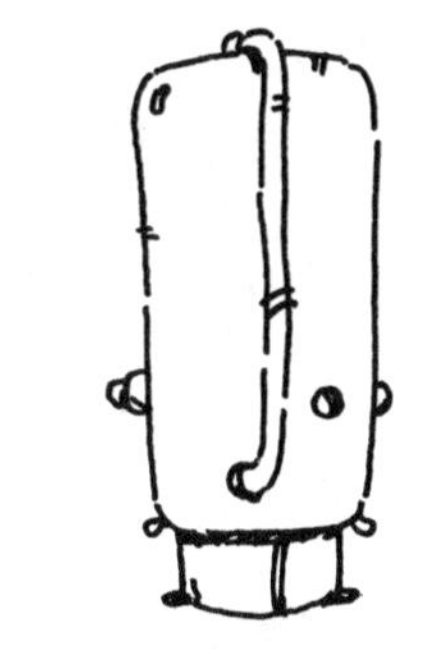

3. Fermentation, fining and racking of the fully fermented wines occur in large, temperature controlled tanks.

4. Wines are aged often for years in special wood aging barrels or steel tanks. The beverages settle out and mature in flavor and character through these quiet hours.

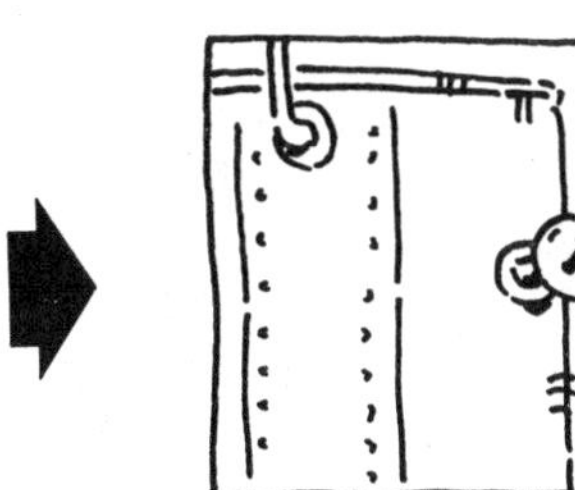

5. Final blending, racking, filtering and cold stabilization of wines and brews takes place immediately before bottling.

6. Modern packaging for wines ranges from the tiny 6 ounce glass bottle to 1,800 ounce plus bulk wine containers. Unpasteurized wines may continue to develop new and pleasing characteristics for years in the bottle.

And For The Two Classic Methods In Sparkling Wines

1. Methôde Champenoise sparkling wines involve a secondary fermentation within the actual bottle that will be sold in the retail store. The wine lies in contact with the lees from the second fermentation for extended periods creating unique and interesting flavors.

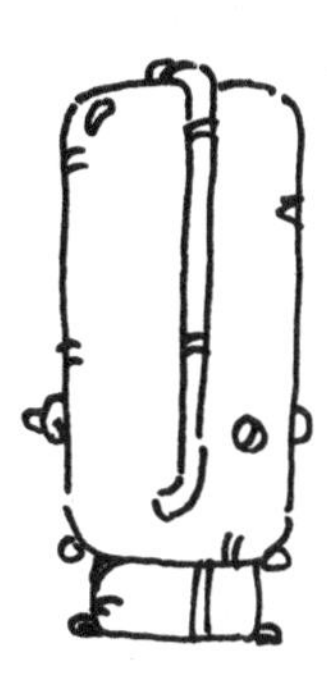

2. The Charmat or Bulk Fermented wines involve a secondary fermentation in large tanks. The newly bubbly wines are separated immediately from the lees, cleaned up, and bottled. These sparkling wines yield a cleaner fresher characteristic more akin to the original still wines used for the secondary fermentation.

Nature produces all of these and many other elements artlessly. The art lies in man's control of fermentation to produce wines which are perceived to be better and the best. Literally thousands of books and hundreds of thousands of scientific articles in dozens of countries have chronicled man's attempts to artfully improve upon nature's gift. However, of all the great scientific breakthroughs in western culture, none had greater significance to modern man's well being than Pasteur's studies on wine fermentation in the last century. In fact, nearly all of modern medicine and the field of microbiology grew from those studies.

So, aside from a tasty and highly romanticized alcoholic beverage, the perfection of the wine art has penetrated nearly every phase of modern life. Quite a legacy for the ubiquitous and miniscule yeast cell.

PATIENCE IS THE ESSENTIAL ATTRIBUTE OF THE WATCHFUL CELLARMASTER (The Wine Institute)

Ford's Easy Outline For Brewing And Spirit Distillation

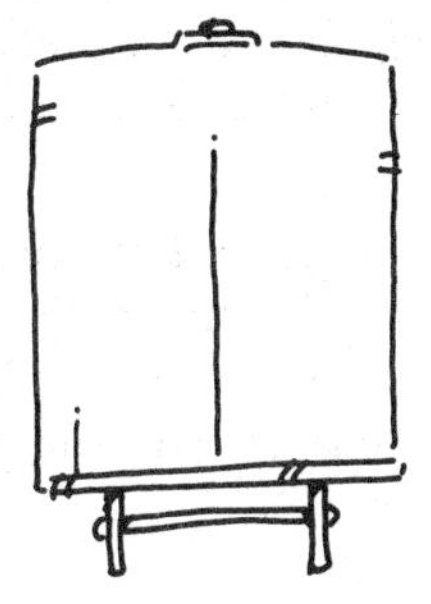

1. Germination or malting of grains is a natural enzymatic step in which the starches are converted to maltose sugar. Maltsters use water and heat on malting floors or in closed containers to induce this natural step. Heat dried to various darknesses, the malts are ground and sold to the brewer and distiller.

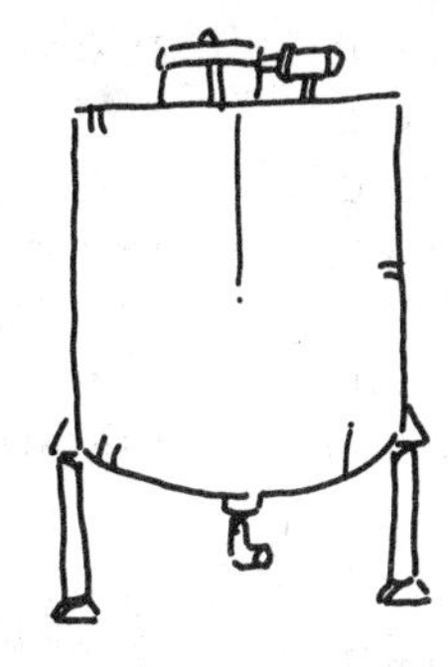

2. Brewing involves the boiling of the malts, and often other grains, to convert more starch to sugar and to flavor the worts with hops. The resulting watery mass contains sugars and flavors ready for fermentation.

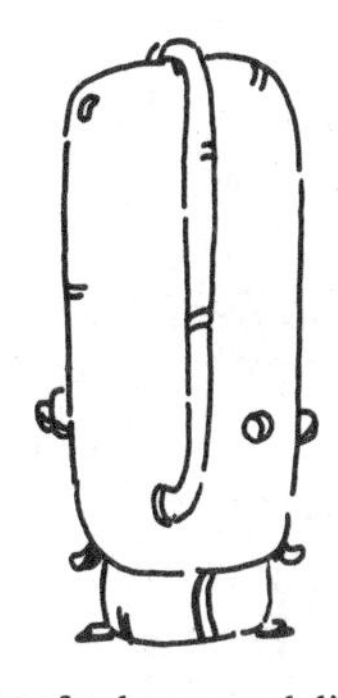

3. Fermentation for brews and distilled spirits occurs in large temperature controlled fermenters, similar to those employed in wineries. The wort yields alcohol at a slightly lower conversion rate than occurs in natural fruit mashes. Brews made for beer are stored for several weeks in cool cellars, the lagering period, before another infusion of carbon dioxide and bottling for sale. Beers have limited shelf life, and should be consumed within weeks of purchase.

4. Brews made for distillation are placed either in small, pot bellied stills for traditional beverages like cognac, or in the huge, double column steel towers that produce most of the world's popular drinking alcohols. In both, intense heat is employed to separate that alcohol and certain portions of other taste congenerics which create the flavors for the various types of spirits.

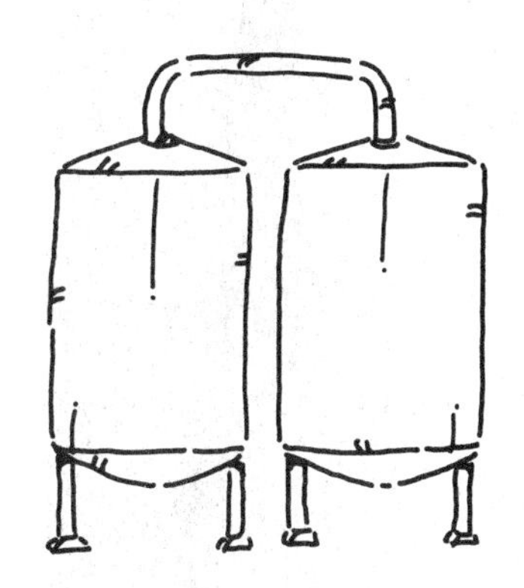

5. Distilled beverages should be aged, most often in wood. The length of aging is the single most important criterion for quality, as these flavor congeneric require long oxidation to mellow out. When finally bottled, the aging process ceases and the product remains inert until the capsule is removed for consumption.

And For Liqueur Maceration, Percolation And Re-Distillation

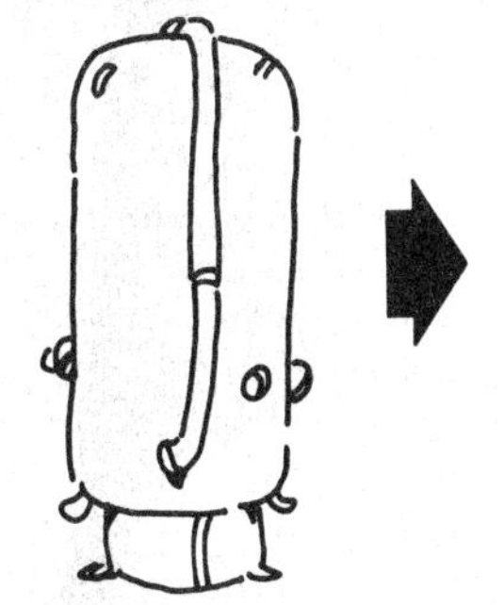

The wondrous and varied flavors in liqueurs and other compounded spirits derive from the same procedures that make coffee, tea and flavored juices. Flavoring agents ranging from herbs and leaves to fruit rinds and dairy creams are soaked, heated, ground, pulverized, blended and even distilled a second time over common spirit bases such as brandy or vodka. As with other spirits, aging ceases and flavors are sealed at bottling.

Acesence

Before Pasteur, many wines spoiled because of acetic acid — just plain vinegar to us. This omnipresent bacteria oxidizes the wine alcohol producing vinegar. If you detect acesence in the odor, the wine likely is over the hill!

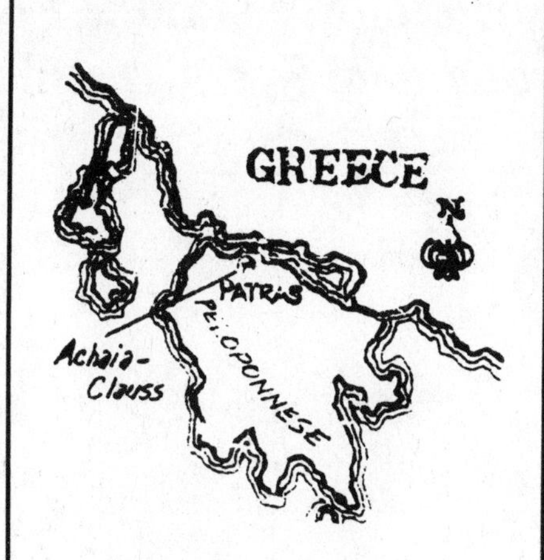

Achaia Clauss

The Greeks have never much taken to regulations, so grapes are grown in a profusion of styles around their many Islands. The best wines consequently are selected by a few large bottlers such as the famous Achaia Claus. Look for their label for fine dry whites.

Aftertaste

A critical step in judging wines and liquors is found in the lingering presence in the throat *after swallowing*. It can range from a gentle fragrance to unpleasant burning. The mouth and throat warm the fluids on the way through releasing brand new tastes and smells.

Aleatico

Travelers to Southern Italy rave over the delicious rose' wine called Aleatico which is served as a liqueur after the meal. The rich Moscato type grapes are stored and dried like raisins for fermentation in the spring. The wines are fragant and sweet desserts in themselves.

Alicante Bouschet

Alicante Bouschet is one of the many hybrid grapes developed in France. A cross of the Grenache and Petite Bouschet, it is one of the few *red juiced* grapes. This deep coloration allowed prohibition mobsters to stretch the wine by adding sugar and water in fermentation.

Alsatian wine

A seventy mile strip of land in Alsace has produced fine wines for thousands of years. The Roman soldiers farmed these producing vineyards. Alsatian wines are nearly always white and made from the riesling grapes popular in neighboring Germany. Unlike the rest of France, the grape varieties are on the label.

Ambrosia

According to the earliest Greek mythology, the gods both bathed in and consumed Ambrosia to gain their strength. The historians believe that ambrosia consisted of very sweet wine made from the rich drippings of unpressed grapes. The modern equivalent is *Tokay Essence,* the richest of dessert wines.

Amontillado

Come to know the treasure of Spain, Amontillado. The fine dry sherries are classified as Fino. The darkest and fullest of these unique blends are shipped throughout the world as Amontillado. Over ice or in a snifter, Amontillado delivers the nutty, fragrant unparalleled aperitif.

Amphora

The graceful, tapering egg-shaped vase popular in ancient Greece was the amphora. An important use of the vessel was the aging of wine. Thus, the Greeks were the first civilized people to know the glories of matured wines!

Angelica

Aside from Zinfandel in the table wines, California can claim a unique wine in Angelica. The concoction is simplicity itself. Pure brandy is blended into fresh grape juice producing by far the sweetest of all drinks. While primarily a cheap, popular wine, there are now a few premium quality brands on the market.

Aperitif

From the Latin *operio* which means *to open,* the appetizer is the light medium dry wine designed to stimulate the appetite before the meal. Often containing quinine and other scented herbs, aromatized wines are vermouths, dry sherries and secret recipes like Dubonnet and Lillet.

Appelation Controlée

French winemakers began to submit to a system of controls in 1855. This highly ordered, strictly classified program is designed to assure a level of quality control in the top ten percent of French produced wines. Rigid control is exercised over types of grapes, amount produced and geographic origin. Look for the words on the label!

Appetizer Wines

Appetizer equals aperitif! Both refer to the light, aromatic wines designed to stimulate the appetite before the meal. Ranging from very dry to moderately sweet, they include the sherries, the vermouths, Madeira and even flavored Marsalas. To your health!

Astringency

Astringency is often confused with bitterness. They go together often but are quite distinct. The phenolic compounds from the skins in red wines cause both sensations. Bitterness is one of the four true tastes, while astringency is a feeling created by the puckering in the mouth. Astringency accompanies pronounced bitterness!

Auslese

The German winemaker specializes in selective late picking as the grapes develop increasing concentrations of grape sugar. The word Auslese means selected. It is the second of four stages of late harvesting and always produces a markedly sweet wine.

Bacchus

Bacchus was one of the more famed gods of mythology who's responsibility was fertility in nature. Great feasts and celebrations called Bacchanalia were held in his honor in both Athens and Rome. A son of Zeus, Bacchus spread the wine culture throughout western civilization. Here's a salute to wise old Bacchus!

Barbaresco

The widely grown *Nebbiolo* grape makes some of Italy's most famous wines including the robust *Barolo.* For a real delight, search out *Barbaresco*, produced in a scant ten thousand case vintage each year. Softer, earlier maturing and less tannic, Barbaresco is Italian red at its best!

Barolo

Italy's biggest, and probably best red wine is harvested in the centuries old tradition and transported in wooden carts to the winery. Barolo emerges from the fermenters as a huge, tannic red that will last for years and years. Fortunately, over 300,000 cases are produced annually. Plan this one with a roast or steak.

Barossa Valley

Barossa

The best known Australian wine area lies in the heart of the state of South Australia. Roughly equivalent to the Napa Valley in length and breadth, the picturesque, rolling land of the Baroso was settled by Germans familiar with wine making. Famous for Rhine-Riesling, the Barossa also yeilds fine shiraz, cabernet sauvignon and grenache wines.

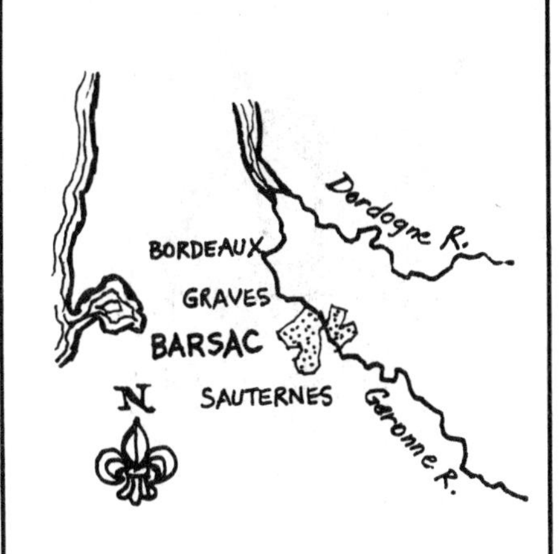

Barsac

If you seek the ideal dessert wine with a touch of the 'noble rot,' seek out a Barsac. The northern area of the Sauternes district in Bordeaux, all Barsac may be called Sauternes but often they do not carry that familiar designation. Less than 200,000 cases are made of these delightful Barsac delights.

Beaujolais

A variety of wine developing great new popularity is the mellow, fruity, young Beaujolais. In its native area south of the great Burgundies, the Gamay grape matures early and, unlike most reds, needs little aging. It's a good beginner red!

Nouveau Beaujolais

One of the most charming events of the tradition laden wine industry occurs with the first sale each fall in France of Nouveau Beaujolais. The lightest of the light reds may be sold on November 15th, scant weeks after fermentation. There ensues a frenzied race to deliver the product in London bars!

Premieur Beaujolais

At midnight plus one minute, on November 15th, French wine law allows the first release of the delightful young red wine called Beaujolais. This first blush is scarcely a month in aging and is light and delightfully fruity. Another month will pass before the full vintage may be released for sale!

Beaune

The charming walled city of Beaune lies in the midst of the famous French Burgundy district called Cote de Beaune, part of the Cote d'Ore. With a scant 1,300 acres of wine grapes, some of the world's greatest deep red wines are found such as Clos de Mouches and Clos de Roi.

Beverage Consumption

It will come as no surprise that Americans have chosen soda pop their favorite beverage — at thirty four gallons per person each year. Other close favorites are coffee at thirty two, milk at twenty four and beer at twenty nine gallons. Meteoric wine, the least consumed at slightly over two gallons, has doubled in the last decade and will soon bypass distilled spirits. Wine is on its way!

Egri Bikaver

Most wines of any distinction from Austria and Hungary are light and white, as their German neighbors. One exception which is in distribution around the world is the velvety, inky dark red wine commonly known as Bull's Blood. Produced near the small town of Eger, this full bodied red is the match of many western European Pinot Noirs.

Black Rooster Legend

The Political League of Chianti has used the Gallo Nero — black rooster — as a symbol since 1200. Legend says the borderline between Florence and Siena was settled by having two men walk until they met at the crack of dawn. The wily Florentines chose an ill fed scrawny black rooster which woke their man first thereby gaining the most territory!

Blanc de Blanc

This phrase in French is translated *white on white.* In practice, it refers to a small amount of French Champagne produced from the white skinned chardonnay grape exclusively. It is a lighter and more expensive cuvee. The vast bulk of Champagne is produced from red grapes with a bit of Chardonnay for style.

Blanc de Noir

It is a surprise to some that French Champagne, nearly always white, is produced from black skinned grapes. The fresh grapes are carefully picked over to eliminate impperfect fruit and gently pressed to release the white pulp for fermentation. Hence *Blanc de Noir*, or white wine from black grapes!

Bocksbeutel

A favorite canteen of the early German housewife was made from leather in the shape of an organ of a goat. By the middle of the 18th Century, the familiar pouch was designed in glass. Today it contains the famous green-eyed gold Steinwein from Germany as well as the popular Rose types from Portugal.

Bodega

Bodega is Spanish for storehouse. Far from prosaic store rooms, the bodega for aging Spanish sherry is more akin to a cathedral with its vaulting roof line and stunning white exterior. Fine sherries are born, age and mature for hundreds of years in these wine churches!

Bordeaux Wine

Simply, Bordeaux is the most important wine region on earth. This small geographic confluence of two rivers in Southern France was cultivated to the vine before Christ by the Romans. Thirty million cases — mostly red cabernet — are produced annually from less than 500 thousand acres. There are over 2,000 named Chateaux in Bordeaux!

Bourgueil

If you cannot locate your favorite Beaujolais, pick up a Bourgueil or a Saint-Nicolas de Bourgueil from the Loire Valley near Touraine. These soft reds employ one of the Bourdeaux grapes, the Cabernet-Franc which matures into a delightful, medium bodied vintage.

Brandewijn

A precious cargo in the Middle Ages from southern France to Holland was marked *Brandewijn.* At this time, an enterprising sea captain boiled out or concentrated the wine intending to add water again at his destination. His customers preferred the distilled spirit called *brand* or burnt wine, a word anglicized to *brandy.*

Breed

One of the most difficult tasks in life is to describe things we taste. The wine connoisseur must employ poetic license to capture the delicate nuances of a particular vintage. However, whether in horseflesh or in good wine, breed is easily understood as the class of the field. A wine of great breed has delicacy, finesse and great character.

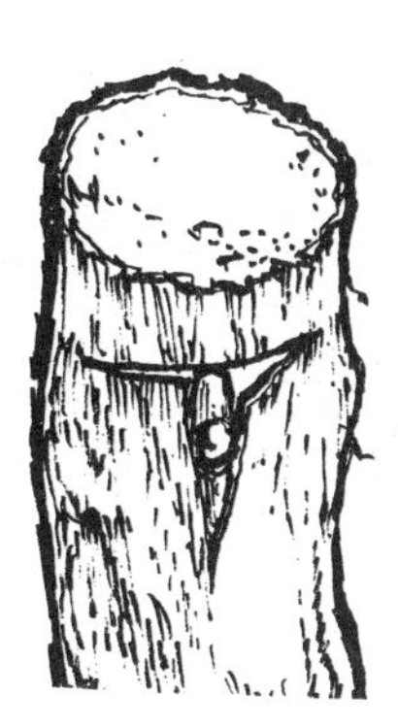

Budding

For many years, orchardists working with citrus and deciduous trees have utilized a unique technique involving the implantation of large buds in a T like cut in the bark of mature trees. The present craze for white wines is causing many California grape growers to *T-Bud* white varieties on red grape wines.

Bumper

The intensely traditional French Catholic through the centuries offered the first drink of wine to the Pope or the 'good father.' In French, the words for 'good father' are *bon pere* which to the American sounded like *bumper*. Hence first drinks became bumpers!

Bunny Foiler

Rabbits love the tender young shoots and leaves of newly grafted grape vines. However, rabbits will not touch the waxy and slippery sides of the common milk carton. Hence, for their first season, most young vines are encased in protective 'bunny foilers'!

Calories in Wine

Dry table wines (those without sugar) average 25 calories per ounce — about 100 calories in a four ounce serving. That compares to about 160 calories in a full glass of milk. Of course, sweet dessert wines have up to 45 calories per ounce!

Castelli-Romani

There must be enormous quantities of common wine for a country that consumes over thirty gallons per person annually. Around the ancient city of Rome, this everyday jug wine is termed Castelli-Romani. It comes in both red and white and often has a taste of sweetness.

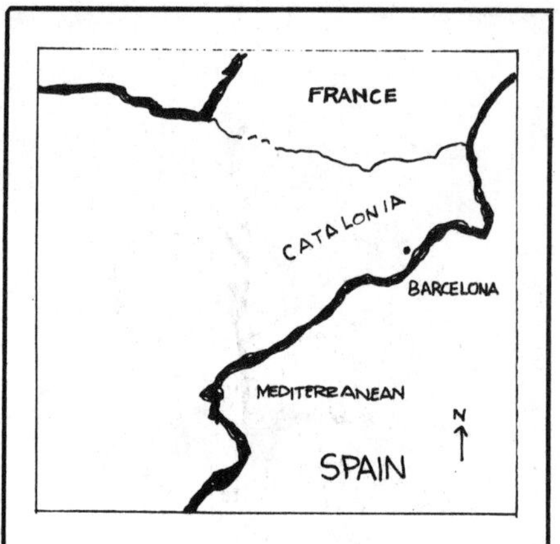

Catalonia

Most of the fine Spanish table wines imported in great numbers in recent years come from the verdant Northeast corner of Spain. Three sub-regions produce distinctive wines — Alella, Tarragona and the Panades. The zesty and inexpensive sparkling wines made in the bottle of fermented French tradition are of outstanding quality.

Chablis

The most distinctive of all white wines is Chablis. True Chablis from the region in Northern France is the most delicate, flinty dry wine of all — the perfect companion of a fish entree. Produced exclusively from the Chardonnay in France, it is imitated world wide and made in many softer, sweet blends. True Chablis, wherever made, is dry and tart!

"To Chambre" a Wine

Wines of great age always have required gentle treatment. The wine steward would bring the fine, long-aged red wines slowly to room temperature — around 66 degrees — before serving. He brought them to *chambre,* or room temperature.

Champagne Sugar Level

Don't let the bubbles fool your taste buds. All sparkling wines contain a dose of sugar added before bottling. A very few French champagnes called Nature are produced without sugar. The sugars by volume in champagnes are: BRUT up to 1 percent; EXTRA DRY up to 3 percent; SEC up to 4 percent; and the real sweet bubbly DOUX and COLD DUCK up to 10 percent.

Champagne Tax

Alas, to the dismay of all true lovers of the bubbly, the federal government grimly holds to its nearly confiscatory champagne tax levied during the second World War. At $3.40 per gallon, the tax is twenty times that of still wine!

Vintage Champagne

The afficionado of vintaged French wines is quite happy to purchase authentic unvintaged champagne. Unlike other classified wines, most champagne is blended from several years and up to forty different wines. Perhaps twice each decade, the harvest is of such superb quality that a vintage champagne is made — a light, delicate and quite expensive bottling!

Chaptilization

In Germany and Northern France, there are often cloudy spells during grape ripening seasons. When this occurs, the fruit lacks sufficient sugar to produce the common twelve percent alcohol wines. Cane sugar is added to produce the alcohol, a practice forbidden in California.

Charcoal Filtering

Charcoal filters have the enviable capacity to remove undesirable elements from fluids. While used generously in whiskey-making, this technique is employed sparingly by winemakers particularly to remove color pigmentation when white wines have rested too long on their skins. Unfortunately, wine character is also lost!

Charmat Champagne

Traditional champagne is produced by a second fermentation in each and every bottle. In 1910 a French winemaker named Eugene Charmat simplified the process by using a 500 gallon steel tank for the second fermentation. Called bulk process on the bottle, Charmat champagne is as good as the wine from which it is made!

Chateauneuf du Pape

The Greeks are credited with planting vines along the Rhone river in Southern France as early as 500 AD. In the Fourteenth Century, the Catholic Popes lived in Avignon and developed vineyards which still produce great wines. These blends of up to thirteen varieties of grapes are big, full bodied and noble reds.

Chevalier du Tastevin

Of all the variety of wine appreciation societies of the world, the 17,000 member Chevaliers are at least the most handsomely costumed if not the most prestigious. Formed in 1934 to promote French Burgundy wines, the group is headquartered in the imposing 600 year old Chateau du Clos de Vougeot. Great and elaborate feasts are staged in the hall with the members arrayed in striking medieval costumes.

Chianti

True Chianti is made only in Central Italy in the Tuscany Province. Grapes used include the Sangiovese, Canaiolo, Trebbiano, and Malvasia del Chianti. All others are sham and imposters! A secondary fermentation (called governo) induced by raisined grapes produces the rich color and matchless taste!

Chieu

It is a surprise to some to learn that the Chinese record wine making more than four thousand years ago. Chieu or Chiew is their all purpose word meaning wine, liquor, brew or liqueur. Persian grape vines were introduced at the time of Christ, but most Chinese "wine" is really brew made from rice and millet seeds.

Cider

Surprisingly, the word cider means different things in different countries. Cider is a pasteurized, soft fruit drink in the United States. It is a quite alcoholic, fermented wine in most other western nations. In France and northern Europe it is often wood aged to a rare drinking form. Check the label when buying *cider*!

Classico

In Italian, the word means classic. Hence, the very best of the Italian vintages — those from very delimited growing areas — may carry the term. You may find Soave Classico or Valpolicello Classico but most often in American markets the famous Chianti Classico.

Colares

The phylloxera plague which nearly destroyed the traditional vineyards of Europe created great popularity with the Colares wines of Western Portugal. Matured in the sandy soils near the Atlantic, these vines were immune from the pest. However, the heavy, tannic tastes of the Colares make them today only interesting, especially heavy reds.

Cold Duck

Produced from a mixture of white and red sparkling wines, cold duck has the highest sugar content of any bubbly wine. Its unique name came about from the corruption of the German words Kalte Ende — meaning the cold end of the evening when all remaining wines were mixed in a toast. A misplaced T created Kalte Ente or Cold Duck!

Commandaria

The world's oldest named wine is luscious, sweet Commandaria from the forbidding isle of Cyprus. Named by the Knights Templar in the 12th Century, it is made by farmers who ferment and age it in pitch lined jars up to a year. It is a tangy, earthy dessert delight!

Consumo

The Methuen Treaty forced Portuguese wines on England over their favorite red Bordeaux. The harsh Upper Douro River wines were quite bitter and unsatisfactory until they were fortified and aged into Port. Today's *consumo* are simply ordinary wines from Portugal.

Consumption

Per capita consumption of wine in our land is somewhat more than two gallons per year. It is growing steadily, particularly among young adults who drink five times the wine as their elders. By contrast, the French, Italians and Spanish exceed thirty gallons per year!

Wine Cork

Pliant, oak bark prevents destructive air from entering bottles so wine will mature. Discovered in 17th century, corked glass replaced barrels and ancient Greek Amphora. If kept wet with wine, corks will last for decades.

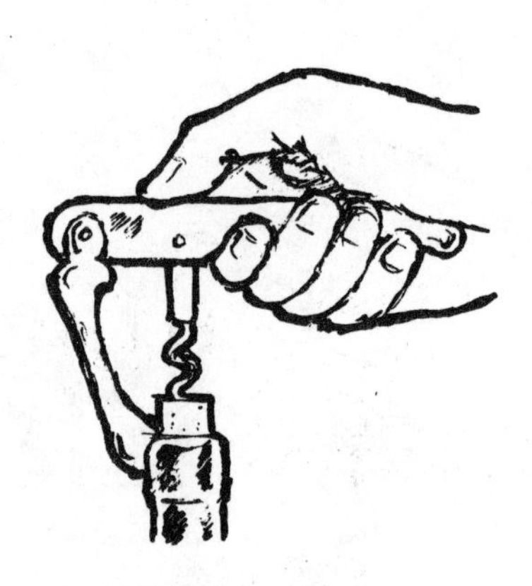

Corkscrew

Though arguments rage back and forth, and enterprising tinkerers continually re-invent new machines, the *waiter's corkscrew* can be depended upon to produce the best results time after time. The narrow, wire-like worm breaks less corks and the leverage in the handle assures a smooth release. It's the best!

Cote Chalonnaise

Look for these red wines for some of the best buys coming from France. Located just to the south of the famous Burgundy vineyards, these lighter red wines still have the finesse and body of the Pinot Noir from which they are made. Look with anticipation for Rully, Givry or Mercurey.

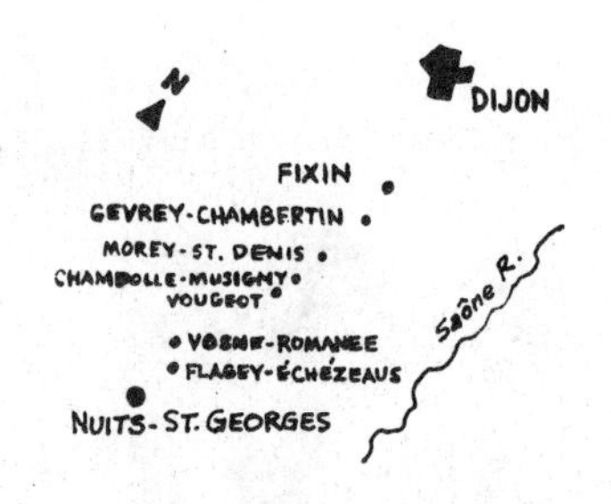

Cote de Nuits

One can hardly conjure in the imagination a twelve mile strip of the earth's crust of the significance of the Cote de Nuits. From the town of Fixin on the North to Nuit St. George on the South, the Pinot Noir grape produces the ultimate in burgundy wines. One can be *sure* with Gevrey-Cahmbertin, Vosne-Romanee and Vougeot!

Cream of Tartar

Aside from the wine itself, fermentation creates a number of useful by-products. None exceeds the ultimate uses of the dominant fruit acid of the grape — *tartaric acid.* Tartar is obtained from the spent husks and pomace and is used in baking powder, in the form of salts for photography and in the form of acid for flavoring. Another wonder of the grape!

Criadera

The enterprising Spanish long ago developed an aging system in which wines from each new year were blended thoroughly to produce the magnificent sherries. The uppermost barrels are all called criadera — or nurseries. Passing down each year, the bottlings are taken from the bottom barrels called the solera. Thereby the Spanish Sherry you drink could have some molecules hundreds of years old!

Cru

Don't be confused by the French designations Cru and Cru Classé. A cru is literally a growth or an agricultural yield from a plot of land. Therefore a good cru is a great growth. However, when shown on a label from the Bordeaux growing region with the word classe, the phrase means a specific classified vineyard.

Crusted Port

Port wine lovers throughout the world recognize the unique designation of a *Vintage Port,* one of selected grapes of extraordinary value which has been *aged in the bottle* up to ten years. Look for an even greater value in a *Crusted Port,* a wine treated the same way from somewhat lesser grapes. Be careful to decant slowly.

White Crystals on Corks

Most wineries today place their wines in refrigerated rooms for up to three weeks before bottling to precipitate wine solids such as potassium bitartrate. Wine bottles stored too long in cold places can develop these harmless tartrate crystals on the corks. Don't worry, its just cream of tartar!

Dégorgement

The French or traditional method of champagne making requires the secondary fermentation to take place right in the bottle. A skilled artisan is needed to disgorge the resulting sediment from the neck of the bottle. The material is frozen in brine and popped out like an ice-cream bar! Wine with sugar is then added and the bottle is recorked for sale.

Degree Day

In grape growing, the degree days are a summation of the daily temperatures ranging above 50 degrees Fahrenheit. The vine does not mature below that level. The average degree days determine the type of grapes to be planted.

Denominazione Di Origine Controllata

In imitation of the French system of quality control, the Italian government established in 1963 their "Controlled Denomination of Origin." Strict standards of grape production and wine making are imposed on those special wines. There are three levels: *Semplice* for ordinary wines; Controllata for wines under special controls and *Garantita* for the finest Italian wine.

Deutsche Weinstrasse

The German Wine Road meanders along the Rhine River from Bockenheim to the Wine Gate at Schwigen on the Alsace frontier. With the Haardt Mountains as backdrop, this strip encompasses some of the most beautiful scenery in the Western world. It also includes the largest wine production in Germany — hence the Weinstrasse!

Diatomaceous Filter

A prehistoric single celled algae provides an ideal filtering agent to bring wines and beers to the consuming brilliance preferred by Americans. The fluids are passed through this coarse, dust-like filter emerging clear of particles, satisfying to the eye and the taste buds!

Doux

The least popular of the French Champagnes goes by the name Doux — meaning sweet in French. The majority of Champagnes contain some concentration of the sweet, natural grape sugar called a 'dosage' added just before final corking. In Doux, the sugar level is at a very high ten percent.

Egrappage

For centuries, fair damsels in French Bordeaux and Burgundy regions patiently separated grape from stem — to speed up fermentation and lessen the bitterness. This *egrappage* now is done by less pretty machines!

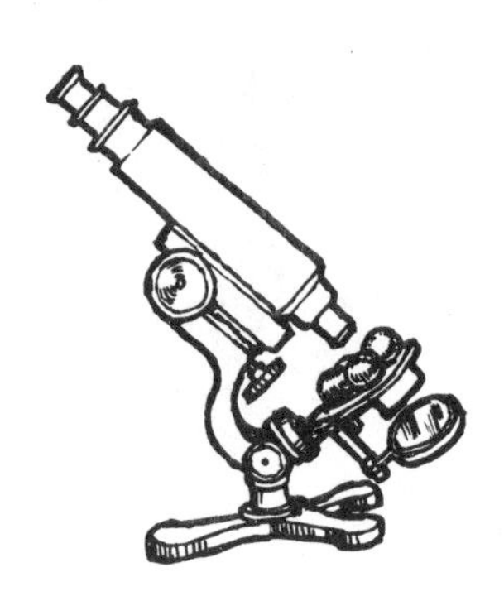

Enology

Enology (oenology) is the science of wine making. It is the chemistry of vinification — man's control of the whims of nature. The enologist harmonizes science with art to produce flawless vintages. He is the little old winemaker!

Grape Enzymes

A very special place in winemaking history is reserved for Louis Pasteur for his discovery of the action of enzymes in grape must. These miniscule protein molecules trigger the complex chemical processes as grape sugars become ethyl alcohol and carbon dioxide. As many as twelve enzymes set in motion dozens of changes similar to the original creation of sugar in the vine. A symphony of nature!

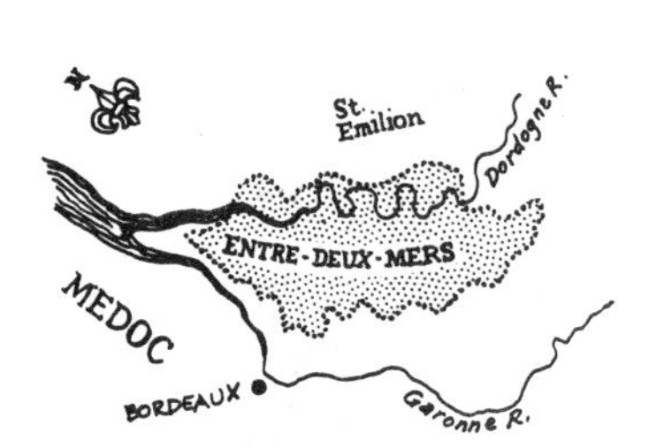

Entre-Deux-Mers

The translation *between two seas* literally refers to two rivers but more appropriately would apply to the sea of Bordeaux wines around Entre-Deux-Mers. Mostly white wines are produced in this 3200 acre section of little distinction. But what neighbors — St. Emilion, Pomerol and Medoc!

Enoteca

The Italians for years have called wine displays Enotecas — from the root word for the making of wine. Literally, any display of wines from anywhere applies. With the new popularity of Italian imports, an official Enoteca in New York City has opened containing over 2,000 different samples of Roman wines.

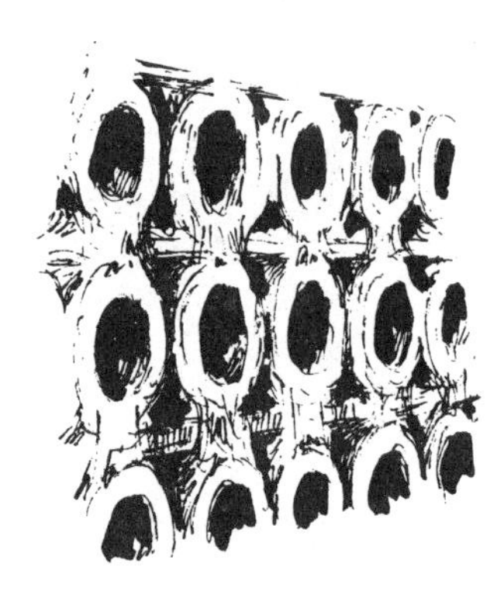

En Tirage

The charm and unique taste characteristics of French Champagne derive from the slow, secondary fermentation *en tirage* — in the bottle. From two to four full years, the wine intermingles with the yeast cells liberating nutrients and essences which create the tastes. Look for the delicate yeasty finish.

Epluchage

One of the reasons that French Champagne maintains such high market acceptance is that the winemakers are intensely selective about the quality of the grapes. In a step called *epluchage,* the harvested grapes are picked by hand saving only the best bunches.

EST! EST! EST!

Perhaps the most romantic of all wine tales was created by a servant who found a semi-sweet Montefiascone wine from Central Italy indescribably beautiful. His employer Bishop sent him ahead with instructions to write on the walls of taverns the condition of the wine served. Overwhelmed, he wrote: IT IS! IT IS! IT IS!

Estate Bottled

As it became necessary through years to distinguish the better classes of wines, the concept of Estate Bottling developed. In a literal sense, estate wines must be grown on the land in which the winery is located and vinified by that firm. Practically, it means wines in which the winery takes great pride.

Esters

While man is limited to four tastes he can readily distinguish hundreds of aromas. The esters in wines provide a profusion of distinct odors ranging from lilacs to green apples. These esters are compounds formed of acids and alcohols and they often change in aging and in the glass during consumption.

Estufa

The estufa or heated warehouse on the isle of Madeira is man's imitation of the hold of a sailing vessel. In Colonial times, the wine of Maderia was treasured for its smooth, aromatic finish which resulted from months at sea in tropic waters. The estufa is simply a heated warehouse in which the young wine cooks and ages!

Fermentation

Through all centuries men were mystified at the function of winemaking. Louis Pasteur found the answer in the middle of the last century to be small, airborne plant life now called yeasts. These *ferments* break down the molecules of fruit or grain sugars creating ethyl alcohol and carbon dioxide. Voila wine or beer!

Malolactic Fermentation

A perfectly natural secondary fermentation occurs in wines, either in the cask or often in the bottle. A common bacteria, changes malic acid to lactic acid creating extra carbon dioxide bubbles. It is particularly desirable in some wines like the popular Lambrusco.

Fining

As early as the Roman period, vintners discovered that wines would clarify during the aging process with the addition of egg whites or skim milk. The process continues today in many wineries, though the centrifuge and modern filters often suffice. These agents literally absorb the suspended solids as they float to the barrel bottom. Clear wines are *fined* wines!

Fleurie

In the heart of the famous Beaujolais zone of eastern France lies the quaint and sleepy town of Fleurie. The word means flowery, and the soft, aromatic young red wine of Fleurie earns its name. Try this flowery young Beaujolais with confidence!

Flor

The delicate, nut-like flavors of Spanish dry sherries derive from a unique, filmy yeast called flor. As if by magic, it forms in December in certain of the aging barrels. From these select barrels come the great fino and amontillado sherry wines.

Frascati

The Italians call it *il sole nel bicchiere* — the sun in a glass. Such is the esteem for the most popular table wine in and around Rome. Produced primarily from two abundant local grapes — Malvasia and Trebbiano — Frascati is a white wine made both dry and semi-sweet. Try this bottled sunshine soon!

Frizzante

Ask an Italian the meaning of frizzante and he will likely answer Lambrusco! The French call it pettillance and we term it sparkle. All refer to the slight carbonation in a beverage that delights the tongue. Lambrusco wine preeminently embodies this brush of effervescense.

Frontingnon

Many a Roman overlord gazed with satisfaction on the abundance of the wine harvest in Frontignon. This sun blessed, vacation spot in Southern France has produced delectable, sweet white wines as much as a thousand years before Christ! You might recognize them as *Muscat de Frontignon.*

Fruity Wine

The most elusive quality in wine tasting is fruitiness. The easiest distinction lies between the young and old. The young wines are more reminiscent of the original fruit, are generally fruitier. Older wines develop bottle bouquet.

German Harvest

Though it is difficult to imagine in the cold German climate, a wine harvest occured as late as the 12th of January in 1980 at Scharlachberg in Bingen. This Eiswein (ice wine) had over thirty percent sugar at harvest. A unique treasure of 100 cases.

German Lage

Since so many German wines are found on American shelves, the wine Afficiando should learn the basic categories to read the labels correctly. The *lage* in German means a vine yard. An Einzlage consists of twelve acres. A Grosslage is made up of a number of Einzllage, up to 120 acres.

Gewurz-traminer

Gewurz means spicy in German. Gewurztraminer is a delightful variety of the popular German and Alsatian traminer white grape. As its name implies, it nearly always yields a spicy, flowery bouquet and an intriguing, soft finish on the tongue. It is increasingly popular also in California. Try it as an aperitif.

Graves Soil

A forty mile strip of land on the banks of the Gironde and Garonne Rivers contains pebbles as large as eggs. These stony, sandy surfaces provide the perfect condition for wide ranging root structures in the vines. Hence, the designation as *Graves* which means gravel in French!

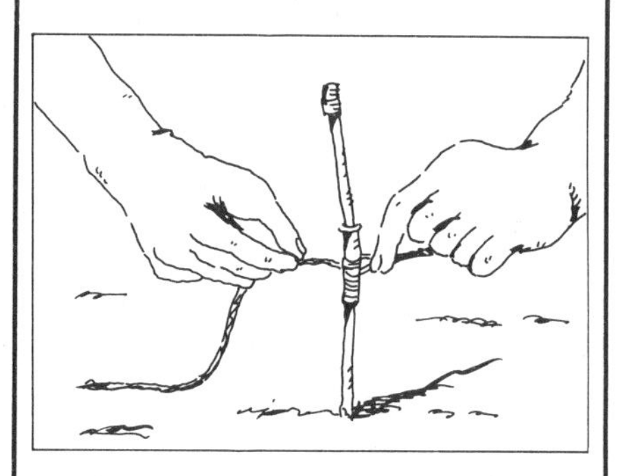

Grafting

In the last half of the nineteenth century, a grapevine plague caused by a burrowing mite called the *phylloxera vastatrix* threatened the existence of all grapes in the western world. Since American native grapestock was resistant to the aphid, the practice grew of grafting all new vineyards on American roots — a practice still used today!

Gout de Terroir

The French have a word for everything, particularly to describe their favorite wines. *Gout de Terroir* literally means the taste of the soil, and many wines gain complexity because of the deep vine root structures in particular soils.

Governo

The gastronomically inventive Italians long ago perfected a system for producing zesty, high alcohol, high tannin wines to complement rich pastas. Called the governo in Chianti wine making, it involved a second fermentation in December from grapes dried on huge trays. For the paisano, it is *vin ordinaire, extra-ordinaire!*

Grappa

Leave it to the little old winemaker to make use of leftovers! A little water and a little yeast added to the pomace or squeezed grape skins will make a strong wine. That wine distilled into brandy is called Grappa in France or California or Eau de Vie De Marc in France. Wherever, it is fiery, white lightning!

Grape Bloom

Over the centuries, the grape berry has developed the perfect covering to protect its precious fruit and to assist the willing winemaker. Called a waxy bloom, the sticky substance on ripe grapes acts as a sun tan lotion and also as the glue to catch those equally precious yeast cells.

Grape Sugars

Very early in the life of man, wine became a staple food. This ancient accident came about because of the predominance of glucose and fructose in the juice of the grape. Unlike many other sugars produced in nature, these two are instantly fermentable in the presence of yeast. Other more complex sugars are present in trace amounts even in the driest of vintages. But, it is glucose and fructose that make the grape berry so very special!

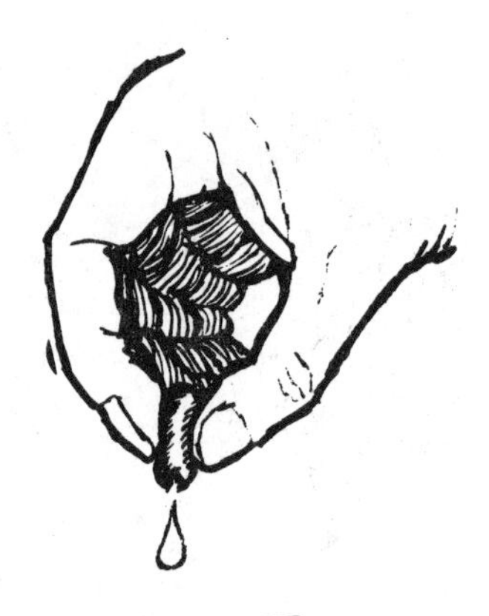

Grape Must

Fresh grape juice is called must by the winemaker. The pulp and the juice alone are colorless and therefore make white wine. For red or rose' wines, the winemaker leaves the skins and seeds in the fermenting tank.

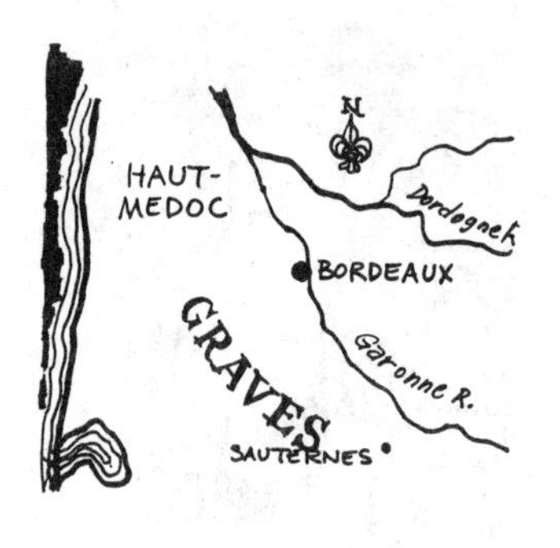

Graves Wine

Novices often associate the Bordeaux area of France exclusively with rich, red Cabernet wines. The forty mile long, twelve mile wide district encompassing Bordeaux city actually produced more whites than reds. Meaning gravel in French, Graves whites are dry, crisp and the match of white Burgundy.

Halbtrocken

German white wines are known for their pronounced level of sweetness, often up to 3 percent of sugar by volume. A new category called halbatrocken — literally *half dry* — can now be found on the shelves. This new category which is half as sweet as the usual German vintage seeks to meet the drier American taste.

Hangover

The French call it wood of the mouth; the Germans call it Katzenjammer or wailing of the cats; in Italy it is Stonato or out of turn. Wherever experienced, overindulgence in beverage alcohol of any form produces both physical and psychological fatigue, headache, and often nausea. Doctors feel a combination of dancing and stress produce the fatigue while toxic congeners irritate cranial arteries. It all can be avoided by moderation!

Agoston Harazthy

Every wine-lover in America should possess a portrait of this far-sighted and industrious Hungarian nobleman. In 1861, he convinced Gov. Downey of California to send him to Europe to procure grapevines. His return with 100,000 cuttings of over 1400 varieties established California's thriving viticulture!

Hectolitre

As the metric system gradually takes over in the United States, it is necessary to acquire a few of the terms that European vintners commonly employ. Most important of these is the *hector or hectoliter* which all of the *appeliation* laws use to restrict production of fine grapes. Remember that a hectoliter equals 26.4 gallons.

Hectare

Now that Americans are getting used to the new metric bottle measurements, can the linear and spatial quantities be far behind? The first to understand is the nearly universal *hectare* vineyard field measurement. Just remember a hectare equals two and a half acres.

Hermitage

Rising majestically, pyramid-like, over the ancient French town called Tain lies a hill called Hermitage. The hill derives its name from a hermit who settled there following a Holy Land Crusade. Hermitage wines, mostly red from the noble Syrah grape, are among the heartiest in the world. Look for heavy tannin and fruity finish.

Hippocras

Long before refrigeration, wines easily spoiled. The thrifty housekeeper solved the problem by mixing the wine with a profusion of fresh fruits and honey. In pouring the wine through a bag of such fruits, enough new flavors emerged to save the faulty wine!

Hospices de Beaune

The charm and grace of the Burgundy area in France is magnificently exemplified in the Hospices or Hospital in the city of Beaune. Built in 1443, the hospital serves the poor of the area benefiting from the sale of wine from its own vineyards. Its famous auction on the third Sunday in November draws wine merchants from all over the world. Look for an Hospices Burgundy soon!

Hothouse Grapes

Perhaps the tiniest of grape wine industries is that in Belgium which began in greenhouses in 1865 as a fresh fruit industry. In the chilly northern European climate, the glass enclosures were necessary to assure ripening. Around 1954, the Belgians began to make small quantities of white wine from red hothouse grapes.

Hotte

Often in Alsace and Germany, vineyards are inaccessible to machinery and animal power. Hundreds of years ago, vineyard workers solved the harvesting problem by developing wicker baskets nearly as large as a man. Strapped to the pickers back, the *hotte* frees the worker's hands protecting the precious cargo.

Green Hungarian

The curious *wine* browser often will find a little known California wine under the curious name of Green Hungarian. The origin of the grape is lost to history, but you can be certain that the bottle contains a pleasant, white wine of neutral flavors. The best bet is to buy one from the coastal riches of California.

Jerez Wine

The Center of Spanish horse racing and bull fighting, the most romantic of all lands, is also the heart of the world of sherry wines. Jerez de la Frontera lies northeast of Gibraltar. Since the middle ages the Palomino grape has been fortified and aged in sun drenched soleras to become incomparable dry Amontillado or luscious sweet Oloroso. Jerez is Sherry!

Jerez de la Frontera

One of the earliest propagations of wine grapes occurred in the lovely Andalusia of Southern Spain. Phoenician adventurers spotted the ideal sun and soil, planted the vines, and called their town Xeres. Jerez — on the frontier — became Sherry to the English.

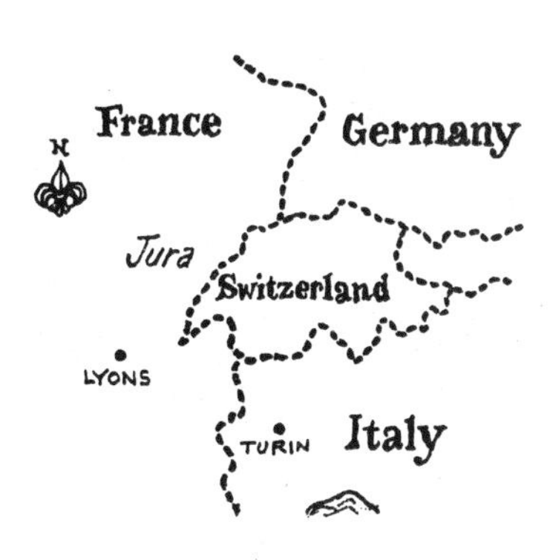

Jura Wines

The very limited wines from this smallest wine region in France are worth the search of your favorite wine shop into the mountains that separate Switzerland from France, the area has but 1,500 acres in grapes — less than some California vineyards! Look for *Arbois Rose'*.

Kiddush Cup

The Kiddush is a blessing recited over wine on the Jewish Sabbath and on holidays. The head of the household chants the prayers in thanksgiving for creation and delivery from bondage. Everyone then partakes of the wine which is usually quite sweet though it may be any type certified by a Rabbi.

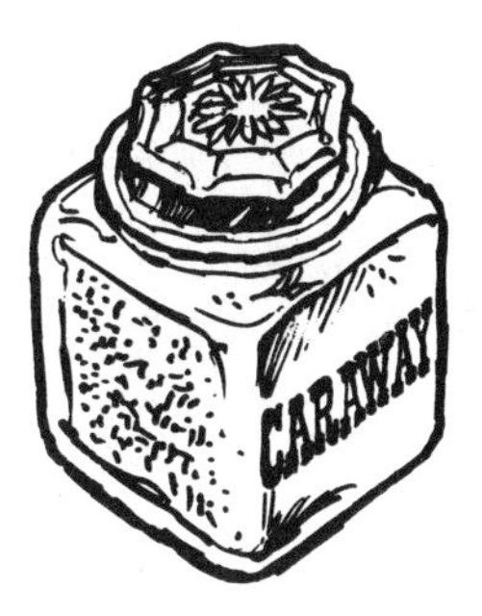

Kummel

A most popular liqueur throughout Northern Europe, KUMMEL (pronounced KIM-EL) is distilled from grain and flavored with caraway and often a dash of cumin. It is pure white, dry to medium sweet and usually sold at 80 proof. Try it after dinner, or as accent to your cocktails.

Kvass

Now that Americans are allowed as tourists in Russia, a new and different beer taste is being acquired. Common both as commercial and home brew, Russian Kvass beer is flavored with mint and cranberries!

Proprietary Label

In the liquor business, a proprietary label is one created by the wine maker or distiller. The ingredients in the bottle may be common knowledge, as in wines, or they may be jealously guarded secret recipes as in Benedictine. No other company may use the name.

Labrusca

The Vikings found a profusion of grape-bearing vines in North America. All were of a common family that readily withstand the coldest of winters called *Vitis labrusca* grapes. Ideal for juice, jam, jelly and luscious as fresh fruit, Labruscas make poor wines. Common types are Concord, Catawba, Niagara and Delaware.

L'Chayim

The Jewish toast to health familiar round the world is L'Chayim. It is given, of course, with wine. The toast celebrates Hebrew Yayin, the wine which Noah made and consumed after the Flood. L'Chayim — TO YOUR HEALTH!

Lacrima Christi

One of the most romantic of all wine tales surround the dry, white golden wines produced from the crumbling lava of Mt. Vesuvius in Tuscany. According to tradition, Lucifer fell from heaven into the Bay of Naples. The good Lord grieved to see the sinful fellow and shed an immortal tear — Lacrima Christi — from which the vineyards grew!

Lambrusco

The Veneto area of North Central Italy has yielded two inestimable gifts to the world — the sausage and Lambrusco wine! From the grape of the same name, Lambrusco is a zesty, fruity, slightly carbonated and nearly always medium sweet red wine. A beautiful beginning red!

Landwein

The newest classification of wine from Germany parallels the country wines of France. Landwein may be produced in 15 distinct regions. Generally they are simple, low alcohol, off-dry versions of lesser quality but pleasant for off-hand consumption.

Languedoc

The world's most productive wine region is encompassed in five districts of the Languedoc in Southern France. Productive, that is, in quantity but not in quality. The base for dessert wines, vermouth and for neutral brandy spirit emerge from this hot and forbidding region.

Liebfraumilch

There is little doubt of the popularity of this light, slightly sweet blended wine from the Rhine River in Germany. It is truly the popular taste. Tradition has the name emanating from the famous church in Mainz called Liebfrauenkirch. More probably it is simply Lieblich which means light, pleasant wine!

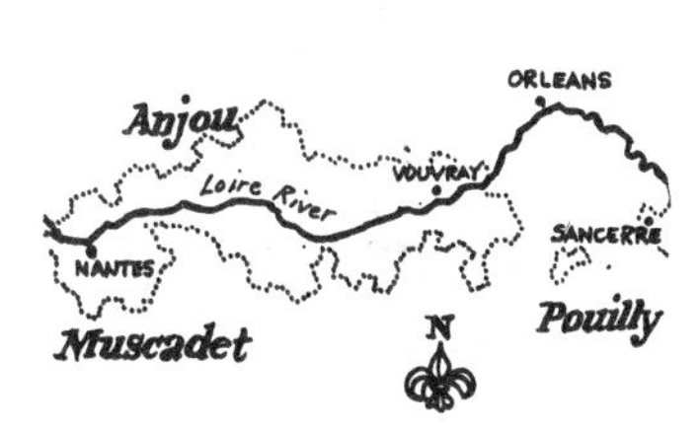

Loire Valley

Running west through the heart of France, the Loire River and its valley provides breathtaking scenery, medieval castles and stunning vineyards. From the dry Pouilly at Sancerre, through the light Vouvray and Anjou Rose' to the salty dry Muscadet, the wines are distinctive and enchanting.

Liter

To lovers of imported wines, the metric system of measurement is well known. In January 1979, all shipments of American wine conformed to these international standards. The liter or about 33.8 ounces is the standard. Three quarters of a liter or 750 milliliters will replace the familiar fifth. The tenth or half bottle of wine will contain 375 milliliters. Very little difference occurs in these smaller sizes but the gallon will be replaced by 3 liters or only 101 fluid ounces. Oh well, we'll get used to it!

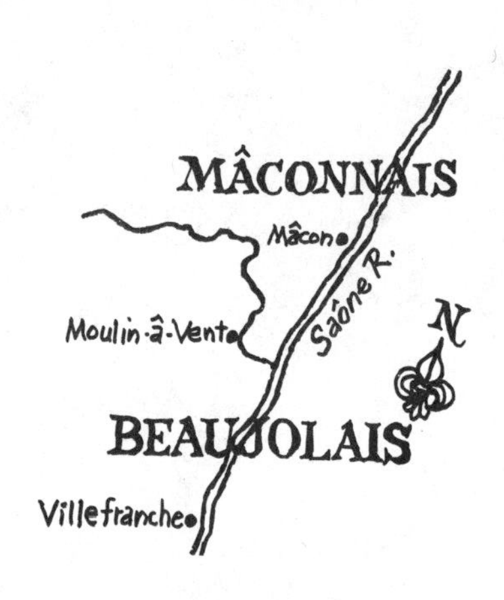

Maconnais

The small Burgundy area to the north of the famous Beaujolais centers around the town of Macon. By far the most famous of these over seven thousand wine acres is Pouilly-Fuisse', a delightful dry white from Chardonnay grapes. Look for the Maconnais label for a good buy in a French white.

Macon Villages

With the strength of the American dollar and the softness of the French franc increasing amounts of undistinguished French wines enter our trade. The Maconnaise section of Southern Burgundy produces not only the famous Pouilly Fuisse, but also many general blends known as *villages* — or from the lands that surround the famed chateau.

Madeira

On a forbidding, volcanic isle 500 miles southeast of Portugal, rugged farmers reap their harvest and carry the grape juice in twelve gallon goat skins to the winemakers. The wines are then stored in heated warehouses for six months producing the longest lived and best of all dessert wines. Madeira! Marvelous Madeira!

Madeira Types

The current revival of fine imported dessert wines includes the craze of Colonial Times — Madeira. These aged, fortified delights come in four distinct styles. Pale dry SERCIAL is the lightest and driest like a fine Sherry. VERDELHO is slightly darker and sweeter. BUOL increases in sugar, a dessert wine. Finally, MALMSEY is rick, full bodied sweet and mellow.

Maderized Wine

Wines — particularly white wines — that show a browning effect are said to be maderized. The causes are often poor storage, exposure to air or simply keeping a delicate white overlong. The true Madeira wine taste by contrast is a desirable baked tang.

Malmsey

Almost from the beginning of Western Civilization, a family of grapes have yielded rich dessert wines over the entire Mediterranean. Of these, Malmsey, the rich, dark brown Mediera pleased both Shakespeare and the Colonial American who prized it with cake.

Malvasia

From its beginnings in Crete to the Atlantic Island of Madeira, the *Malvasia* grape literally captured the palates of Western Civilization. For several thousand years generations upon generations delighted in its mellow, white dessert wines. Today the most popular version is Malmsey from Madeira.

Manzanilla

Still within the Sherry region, Manzanilla is produced in an area twelve miles north of Jerez overlooking the Atlantic Ocean. This very dry, gossamer light sherry seems to incorporate the salt breezes during aging. It is by far the most austere and delicate of the sherry family.

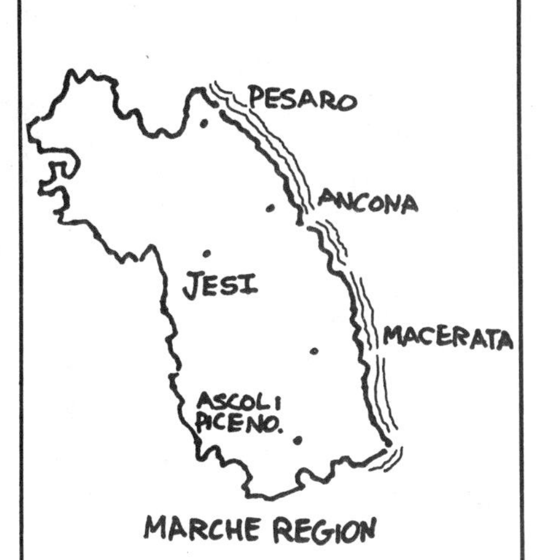

Marche

Though one of the more breathtaking regions in scenery, the Marche area of winemaking on the Italian Adriatic Sea is the least in terms of wines. Least, that is, with the exception of the tart and perfectly dry white called Verdicchio de Castelli di Jesi — a fish wine supreme!

Marsala

The famed and beloved dessert wine of Italy is incomparable Marsala. Though at times found in dry versions, most Marsala is sweet and walnut brown in color with a slight acid undertone. Marsala Speciales are blended with popular tastes such as banana, mocha and strawberry for perfect desserts.

Mastikha

Leave it to the Greeks and their love of resins to produce a liqueur from the Mastic tree which grows on the Island of Chios. Like their popular resined wines, Mastikha is quite dry with a tangy, woody finish.

Mavrodaphne

In 1845 a Bavarian named Gustav Clauss settled in Patros, Greece and founded a winery now world famous — Achaia-Clauss. He produced a rich, muscat-tinged sweet dessert wine called Mavrodaphne. Of immense popularity yet today, myth has it he named it for the love of his life who reminded him of the enchanted goddess, Daphne.

Mechage

Soon after wood barrels replaced the old Roman amphoras, wine began to spoil with great frequency because the wood staves held yeast and bacteria. The practice grew of burning a wick — a *meche* — of sulfur to render the barrel clean before entering new wine. The practice continues to this day.

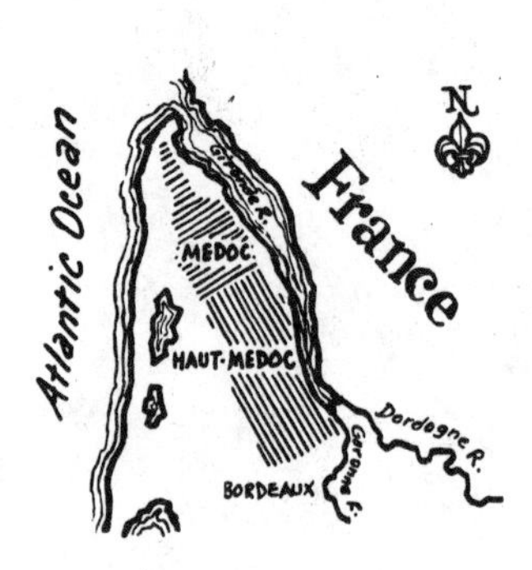

Medoc

For two thousand or more years, grapes for wine have been harvested along the stately Gironde River in Southern France. *The Haut Medoc* Bordeaux region can be termed the best of the best, producing the incomparable Chateaux cabernet sauvignon classified in 1855. Magnifique!

Mercury

To the confirmed wine lover, Mercurey is neither planet nor messenger of the gods but a superbly soft French red wine. Produced from the same Pinot Noir grapes as the famous Beaune vineyards to the North, Mercurey has earned a world-wide acceptance. One bottle will convince you!

Microclimate

Through untold seasons of history, wine grape growers have recorded the absolutely ideal pockets of geography which mature the very best wine grapes. Today, the scientists intensively study the wind, the sun, the soil, the fog, the frost and any other elements that will affect grape maturity. The really great wines emerge from these minute microclimates.

The Midi

The vast stretch of land from the Rhone River in southern France to Spain comprises the Midi. From a sheer production viewpoint, it produces an astounding five percent of the world's wine and nearly a third of France's heavy consumption. Like the arid hot San Joaquin Valley of California, it produces everyday wines in profusion!

Mistelle

Around the Pyrenees Mountains in Southern France, both the French and Spanish viniers produce a luscious, sweet dessert wine by mixing brandy into pure, sweet grape juice used primarily and a vermouth, *Mistelle* is a sipping delight.

Monzelun Oak

Wine literature often extols the virtues of aging fine wine in the Limousin and Troncaise French oaks. A really special quality comes from the heavy deposits of tannin in *Monzelun* oak from Southern France. This black oak is used to age Armagnac.

Moselle Wine

The easiest way to distinguish a Moselle wine is by the dark green bottle. Rhine wines are in similar brown bottles. A better way is to enjoy the charming, light, fragrant and often dry Reisling vintages. A combination of slate soil and crisp, cool climate produces the very best German wines. The prevailing cool climate prompts grape growers to cut back the leaves to catch every ray of sunshine on the terraced sloping vineyards. You'll love the Moselle!

Moulin au Vent

The King of the popular Beaujolais vintages is undoubtedly Moulin Au Vent. The name derives from a stone windmill set amidst the vast fields of grapes. It is a noble, big, Gamay wine and one of the few from the region that ages well.

Muller-Thurgau

Muller-Thurgau is a hybrid grape that literally dominates the vineyards in Germany. A cross between the elegant and shy bearing Riesling and the sharp Sylvaner, Muller-Thurgau seems to be the best of both worlds. Though soft in acid, it is a heavy bearer and provides the base wine for the popular wines including the many Liebraumilch labels.

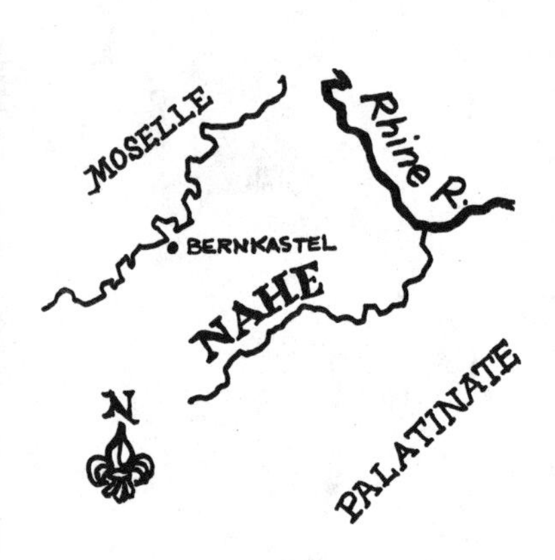

Nahe

Slightly over ten thousand acres — about half of the Napa Valley — are in wine grapes along the picturesque Nahe River, a tributary that leads to the Rhine. An incredible four million cases of wine emerge annually from these productive vineyards mostly of the light and tart Riesling and Silvaner varieties.

Niersteiner

Nearly all wine drinkers in America know the Rhinehessen as the source of the great flood of nice but common wines known as Liebfraumilch. Few have found the gems of this huge producing area, the 1600 acres around the town of Nierstein where the red sandstone supports Rieslings of extraordinary body and bouquet. Look for a Niersteiner with Riesling on the label!

Noble Rot

Noble Rot or botrytis cinerea is a curious variation of the air-born molds that attack ripe grapes. Filaments of the mold penetrate the grape skins without damaging the fruit. The juice is depleted thereby concentrating the grape sugars which will produce luscious, creamy wines.

Oloroso

The word *fino* on Spanish sherry labels refers to the very dry, pale and nutty flavors from a peculiar yeast called flor. The *other* Spanish sherry, quite as popular, is found most often in sweetened versions called Cream Sherry. These Olorosos do not develop flor but are fuller, richer and often more pungent.

Origin of the Aperitif

The Latin word *operio* means to open. Naturally enough, the Romans invented the *aperitif* which was the light, often herb flavored wine drink which stimulated appetite before the meal. Today we call such wines aromatized like the popular vermouth.

Orvieto

Each major wine country developes a favorite white wine for everyday service. Germany has liebfraumilch. Italy has Orvieto produced from a half dozen grapes and sold both very dry as *secco* and sweet as *abboccato*. Look for this pleasant, fruity delight.

Palate

Wine lovers should be particularly thankful for the palate — the bony-muscular separation between mouth and nasal cavity. The hard palate forms the roof of the mouth and the soft creates the throat closure. Both contain sensitive taste buds. Great wines are always *palatable!*

Palatinate

The most Southern portion of the Rhine River has been dubbed the Palatinate since Roman times. Roughly meaning the castle on the hill, the medieval castles imitated those constructed on Rome's seven hills. In early times, this wine-abundant area was termed The Wine Cellar of the Holy Roman Empire!

Palo Cortado

Very rarely produced today, the true *palo cortado* sherry must experience up to twenty years in aging barrels. A cross between the very dry and nutty *fino* and a dry *oloroso,* the wine is crisp and nutty in flavor.

Passerilage

In the torrid Languedoc area of Southern France, there is produced a profusion of rich dessert wines. The objective of high alcohol and high sugar is achieved in a unique grape growing technique. The canes are tied below the fruit to cut the flow of sap from the fruit. The sugar concentrates for the rich, mellow wines!

Passito

Italians enjoy many wines but they satisfy the sweet tooth by producing *passito* from partially dried and raisined grapes. The noble Trebbiano and Malvasia grapes lose nearly all of their moisture producing a rich, mellow, sweet wine similar to the German late harvest types.

Pedro Ximinez

Pedro Ximinez is a variety of grape that sweetens all of the medium dry and luscious dessert wines from Spain. Since the vine bears large, succulent berries, the practice for centuries has been to dry the fresh grapes in the sun. The concentrated juice makes richly sweet wines.

Perry

Every source of fresh natural sugar such as pears or apples were employed as wine sources in Colonial times. European grapes would not survive the winters and the pests and native vines made lesser wines. Perry, from pears, was popular both as a still and a sparkling wine.

Persian Poison

Shah Djemsheed in Persia always kept a bowl of grapes by his bedside. According to ancient lore, one day he found some of his fruit fermented and he marked it poison. A neglected harem girl drank it planning suicide. The gentel intoxication delighted her and she brought her discovery to the Shah. Both lived happily thereafter!

Petite Chateaux

For the serious student of wines as well as the casual buyer, the Bordeaux Petite Chateau can represent the glorious lucky find or a mediocre to unsatisfying bottle. In times of short supply, many of the three thousand or so small vineyards seek market acceptance under their own, unclassified labels. Seek advice from your wine merchant and enjoy the hunt!

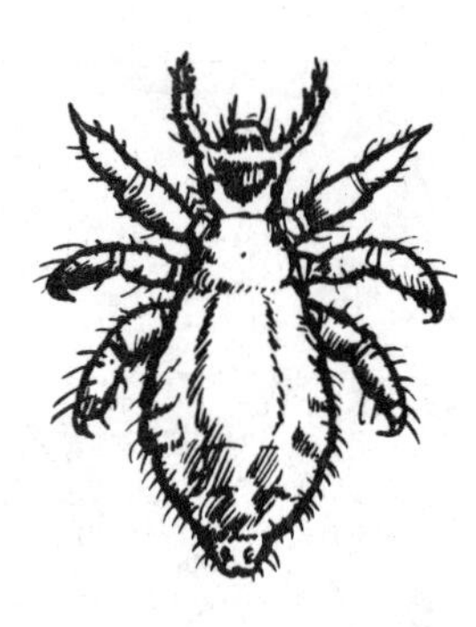

Phylloxera

Phylloxera vastatrix is a native American plant louse of the familiar aphid family. This pesky critter burrows into the tender roots of grapevines literally sapping their energies. It nearly devastated the world's vineyards last century. Now almost all grape types are grafted on hardy, resistant American grape rootstock.

Piquette

Through untold centuries, the wine ration for French vineyard workers has been the Piquette. It is made from a fermentation of water and the discarded skins and pips of the regular vintage. Low in alcohol and high in acid it is a satisfactory bonus and infinitely better than the water!

Pommard

In the very heart of the Cote de Beaune, lies one of the greatest of the French Burgundy wine districts — Pommard. The 850 acres of prime land produce a scant one hundred thousand or so cases of deep red, full bodied Pinot Noir wines. The better Pommard also identify the specific vineyard as in Epenot or Les Cambes. Pommard and quality — *out la meme!*

Porto

O Porto means The Port. Since ancient times this lovely Portugese town has been the center of commerce for the rich, red dessert wines produced in the upper Douro river. First as consumers and later as merchants, the British carried this wine throughout the civilized world.

Tawny Port

Now that ports and sherries are recognized as after dinner delights, the world has discovered the finesse and charm of the noble Tawny Port. Softer, less fruity than Ruby Port, this rich port gains its tawny color from long years of aging in wood. Try it with cheese instead of dessert!

Late-Bottled Vintage Port

Always keep an eye out for an imported Port with a Late-Bottled designation, the great Vintage Ports must be bottle aged after only two years in wood casks. Late Bottled Vintage ports remain in the wood up to four years but require less bottle aging and are less.

Vintage Port

All Port wines are great but few are vintaged. As with French Champagne, only the very best years in Portugal are set aside for individual barrel aging of two to three years. Then these superb, mellow ports are bottled and rest for at least another ten years. Uniquely, both the vintage year and the bottling year show on the label.

Wooded Port

The great Port wine from Portugal is aged in wood in a system similar to the Spanish Solera system. Wine is blended barrel to barrel during aging. The style of each shipper is dominant as these wooded port blends contain as many as thirty different wines. Egg whites are used to clean the wine of sediment every year or so producing drier, tawny colored and luxuriously soft wines.

Pouilly Fume'

The Sauvignon Blanc grape fermented to dryness along the Loire River in Northern France is called Pouilly Fume' because it smells, and almost tastes smokey — fume'. The same grape has become greatly popular in California called Blanc or white Fume'.

Pramnian Wine

The favorite wine of both Nestor and Homer. Pramnian seems to have been a style of wine making more than a single grape product. The early civilizations had few sources to satisfy the sweet tooth — sugar cane did not come to Europe until the Middle Ages. Therefore the most favored wines were the sweetest, probably made from over-ripe grapes. The Nectar of the Gods!

Provence

Wine books and wine lovers rave over the glories of Burgundy and Bordeaux but seldom mention lowly Provence. The glorious sun baked coast of Southern France was planted to grapes by the Phoenecians. Caesar favored its wines. Alas, today the predominantly hot climate produces high alcohol, low acid vintages of little distinction. Provence is, however, the most heavily cultivated grape district in the world!

Grape Pruning

The industrious Romans are credited with the early perfection of this art which seeks to select out a limited number of buds for the following year's fruit. It creates the balance between quantity and quality and is accomplished in mid-winter by skilled craftsmen who cut away the old wood. Great wines come from great pruners!

Quinta

Perhaps the most romantic and difficult terrain on the earth given to grape growing lies amid the upper Douro river cliffs in Portugal. Here the grapes for the reknowned ports are grown in agricultural estates called quintas. Steep, forbidding and dramatically terraced estates dazzle the eye and challenge the grape picker!

Qualitatswein

The range of types and classifications of German wines became so complex and mysterious that a single quality code was adopted in 1971. Eleven regions were designated as Quality or Qualitatswein. In addition each could be further qualified by a *Pradikat.* In ascending order these pradikat are Cabinett, Spaetlese, Auslese, Beerenauslese and Trockenenauslese. Still confused?

Racking

One of the most important steps in producing lively, fruity young wines for today's market is that of racking. The process removes the new wines from their spent lees, yeasts and solids. The step is taken several times through the first year, often after fining with egg white or bentonite to coagulate the solids. Racking makes clean wines!

Rainwater

Often the words Rainwater and Madeira are considered inseparable. The identification came out because of the superior ending and aging skills of one William Neyle Habersham, born in 1947 in Savannah, Georgia. He dated a light, pale blend and aged it for the purity of the rain from heaven.

Rancio

Though the world *rancio* derives from the word for rank or rancid, it has quite a special meaning for this wine. This is the unique quality from long bottle aging.

Rebeche

What happens to the rest of the wine not chosen by the French champagne makers? The second and third pressinigs of this valuable must go to a bitter local wine, or as often to the local still to make a strong version of brandy called *Eau de Vie,* a popular local spirit.

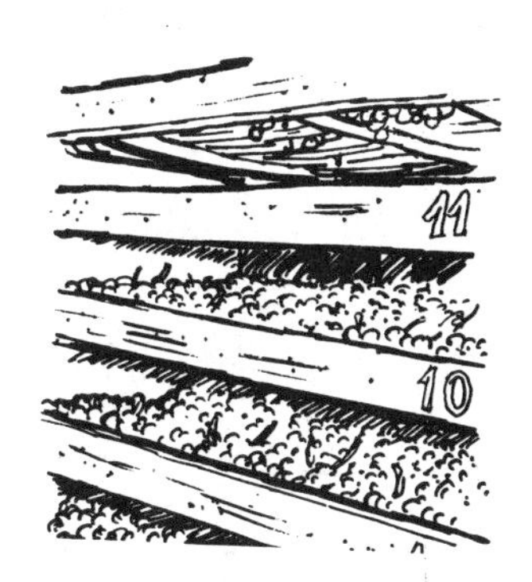

Recioto

A unique process creates Recioto near the beautiful town of Verona in northern Italy. Called passito, specially picked very ripe grapes are placed in shallow, cane bottomed trays to dry until January. A slow fermentation of forty five days is followed by another of eighteen months. The result is, very high alcohol production. It is made in dry, sweet and sparkling versions.

Remuage

Remuage is French for "shaking" and that is exactly what the French do to their bottle fermenting champagne. A trained *Remueur* turns up to 32 thousands bottles in a day, helping to settle the sediment in the neck of the bottle.

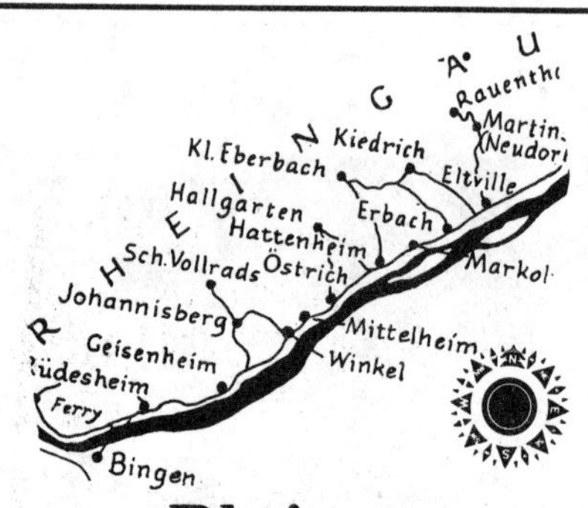

Rheingau

The drama of the medieval castles along the Rhine is surpassed only by the annual joust with nature to pick the grape harvest as late as possible. The superb late harvested Rieslings sometimes as late as December occur in a stretch of the river from Hockheim to Bingen. Protected from the north winds, the grapes grow old and become concentrated in sugar. Over three thousand grape growers produce extraordinary vintages on a scant six thousand acres. Rheingau — Rhine Glory!

Rheinpfalz

The warmest and most productive agricultural area of Germany extends along the upper Rhine, to the French border, and is called the Rheinpfalz. Because the Haardt Mountains protect it from the cold north winds, the area produces many Spaetlese (late harvest) grapes. The wines of the region are soft in flavor, and are the standard carafe drink of Germany.

Rioja

The truly great table wines of Spain originate on the banks of the River Ebro. This northeastern section has a milder climate in both summer and winter conducive to the production of both dry and sweet wines. All three types — Tinto, Blanco and Rose' abound. Look for the Riserva on the label for the best vintages.

Sack

In 1604, James I of England approved the primacy of Spanish sweet dessert wine called Sherris Sack. This was to distinguish the quality of Sherris or Sherry from similar popular dessert wines from Madeira, the Canaries and the Mediterranean. Henceforth to immortality, Shakespeare celebrated *Sack* through the speeches of Falstaff!

Saint-Estephe

The northernmost tip of the famed Haut Medoc in Bordeaux France contains the equally famous Saint-Estephe region. These light red wines grow in clay soils producing both excellent and common growths. The most famous of this region are second *cru Chateau Montrose* and *Cos d'Estournel.* But, be confident with any Saint-Estephe.

Sangria

In Spain, the hot districts of Tarragona and the La Mancha near Madrid, produce undistinguished red wines which come to life in the warming, tart punch called Sangria. The addition of Andalusian oranges and lemons plus apricot and sugar does the trick. Try it yourself with an inexpensive red. Ole and Salud!

Vino Santo

In many European nations, but most particularly all around the boot of Italy, *vino santo* are fermented from dried and raisined grapes. Hung to dry on great racks, the grapes lose their water concentrating the sugars and minerals for sweet, luscious wines which often ferment out to an astounding sixteen percent in alcohol!

Schaumwein

The Germans love the sparkle, consuming an incredible three and a half liters of sparkling wine per capita annually. Most wine lovers recognize *Sekt* as German for sparkling wine. *Schaum* means foam, and much more common foaming wine is produced for local consumption as *Schaumwein.*

Schloss

Part of the charm of European wines lies in the historical settings from which they are produced. The word *Schloss* in German means castle. When you read Schloss Johannisberg or Schloss Vollrads on the label, reference is made to the magnificent, commanding castles of the Rhine River.

Sec

Leave it to the French to confuse you? Sec, which means dry, refers to their champagnes containing 3 to 5 percent sugar! However, on American and other important bottles, sec quite literally refers to wines which have no recognizable sugar content.

Fino Sherry

One of the most charming and mysterious of grape wine stories is found in the development of a special mold called flor on aging sherry wine. Casks which develop these "flowers" are marked and set aside in Spain for the lightest, palest and most delicate of the nutlike fino sherries.

Flor Sherry

In Spain, Flor means flower. One the rarest and most enchanting of the thousands of airborne fermenting yeasts is also called Flor. Found only in Jerez, Spain and the Jura Mountains of France, the yeast settles selectively on some of the aging sherries creating a thick mold. These lucky casks become the matchless, dry and nutty tasting Fino sherries.

Sherry Vintage

The customer who believes vintaging means quality will be forever disappointed in Spanish Sherry. *All sherries are blends* which are freely intermingled from distinct growing areas. Further, the solera system mixes the new with the old wines. Sherry is the triumph of the blender!

Sherry Wine

Since the middle ages, an incomparable sipping and cooking wine has been made in Andalusia, southern Spain. It results from a post-fermentation mold which grows in flowers called FLOR on the new wine. The resulting wine has a baked, nutty character — The Sherry taste!

Soave

No matter the producer, look for Soave from the small town near Verona, Italy as a delightful, clean and sharp white wine. Without doubt, Soave maintains international popularity.

Solera

A common misconception is that aging Sherry barrels are called Solera since they sit in the sun. Actually, the word solera derives from suela meazing ground. Aged sherries are always taken from the ground or bottom barrels which contain mixtures of all the sherries above them.

Sommelier

Literally, the word refers in French to a wine waiter. In early days, this gentleman also kept the keys to the important storage cellars, and performed other important housekeeping chores. The traditional sommelier wears a black jacket and leather apron and has a tasting cup around his neck.

Spatlese

Spatlese in German means *late picking*. It is an umbrella term to cover the many grades of late harvesting of grapes in order to concentrate the sugars to make sweeter, richer wines. In America, these types of wine must be labeled Late Harvest.

Split Bottle

Much confusion exists about a "split" of wine. The split is one quarter of the full bottle. The middle size is termed a half. The new metric bottles use the terms small, medium and regular.

Spritzig

The German like to say that you have moving lips after drinking a slightly fizzy or spritzig wine. Caused by a secondary fermentation after bottling, the very low level of carbonation gives life and vitality to the wine. The word probably derives from the German mixture of wine and soda called a spritzig.

Asti Spumante

In the Piedmont of Northern Italy, there is made a luscious sweet sparkling wine unmatched in the world. Spumante means sparkling in Italian. Asti is the town. Muscat is the grape. They combine to produce a bubbly delight to accompany any dessert.

Sugar-Acid Ratio

Nothing in the romance and ancient lore of winemaking matches the balance of sugar and acids. Winemakers demand and pay highest prices for those grapes picked on the optimum day when these two elements are in perfect harmony. Too much sun respires the precious acids which give the pleasing bite to the wine!

Sussreserve

Suss means sweet in the German language. Since many of the Riesling grapes grown in Germany are excessively tart, a small amount of very sweet grape juice is added before bottling. What the California winemakers calls extract is known as sussreserve on the Rhine.

Tafelwein

Deutscher Tafelwein (literally German table wine) is the light, inexpensive, everyday table wine of Germany like the vin ordinaire of France. The region of origin is usually named and the type of grape that makes up at least 75% of the wine inside.

Taste buds

Nothing is more important or more taken for granted than the mystery of taste. Over ten thousand minute taste buds line the tongue and palate. These nerve endings transmit signals translating into sweet, sour or acid, bitter and salt. Psychologists argue that taste and smell form one harmonious function. A salute to the buds!

Tete de Cuvee

Literally, the tete de cuvee is the top of the barrel. For many years, this phrase was used in France to describe the very best wines, and is still widely used by wine journalists. The phrase was officially replaced in 1935 by Grand Cru, a broader term that can relate both to the wines and the vineyards.

Titration

Every winemaker knows the importance of sufficient acidity in the grape must. Short of the chemistry lab, a simple system of titration evolved for measuring the acidity. A drop or two of an alkai like caustic soda in the grape juice gives simple measure of tartness.

Tokaji Azsu

Tokaji Azsu is the delightful dessert wine of Hungary made from the Furmint grape. Its imitations in the west are called Tokay. The word Azsu means the late gathered grapes which have sweetened and concentrated with noble rot. These Azsu grapes are added to the fermenting wines in pails or puttonys to enrich the blends.

American Tokay

Don't be puzzled by the similarity in names. American Tokay is a pleasant, medium-sweet blend of Sherry and Port with perhaps a touch of Angelica. Additionally, it is strengthened with brandy alcohol. While a fine after dinner toasting wine, it is far removed from the famous white, Hungarian Tokay.

Toast

The practice of toasting is at least one thousand years old. It is said to have begun with the Danes who were fond of quaffing brews in honor of dearly departed friends. By the seventeenth century the toast included dipping rough bread in the wines and liquors for added taste. Hence the toast!

Tonneau

Reports from the famous Bordeaux area of France often indicate shipments in so many hundreds of tonneaux. The word means barrel, the rough equivalent of tun in English. A Bordeaux tonneau is the same as 237 American gallons.

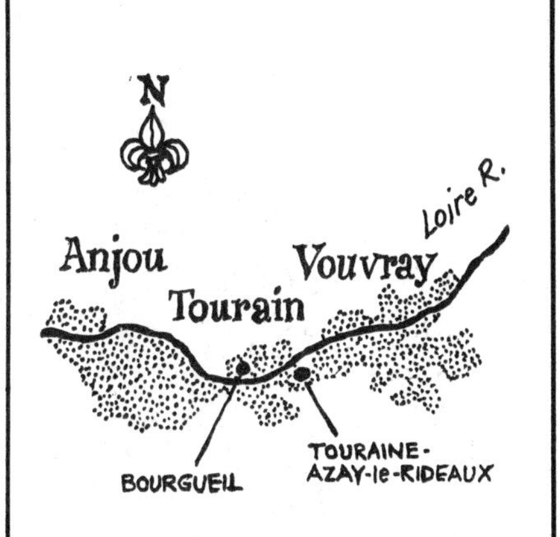

Touraine

If a tourist to France wants both scenery and wine, the Touraine is the only destination. A fairy land of castles next to the meandering, Loire river, the Touraine includes the famous Chenin Blanc wines of Vouvray and Saumur as well as the soft reds called Chinon and Bourgueille.

Traminer

Originally from the Italian Tyrol, this white grape with a pinkish skin now predominates in the Alsace of France and the Rhine of Germany. A clone of the mother grape that produces a spicy odor and taste has been renamed Gewurztraminer. This aromic version is popular in Alsace and in California.

Trockenbeer Enauslese

Perhaps the most difficult to pronounce German wines is most certainly the most luscious of all. Very late harvesting of individual sun-ripened, shriveled berries — that's what the word means in German — creates high sugar, unbelievably mellow wines. Phonetically, its pronounced: TROKE-EN-BEER-EN-OUS-LAY-ZAH.

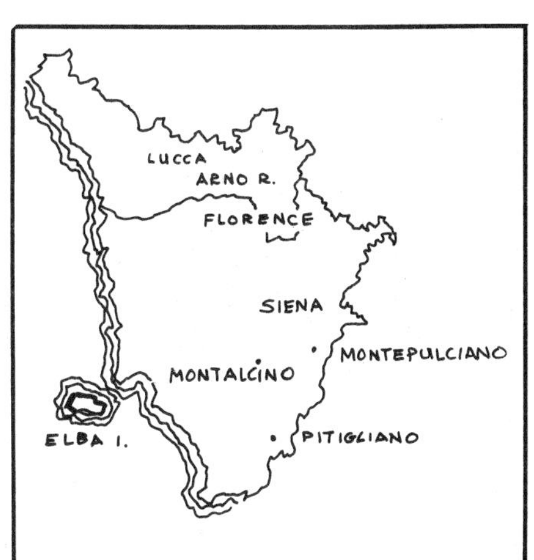

Tuscany

The province of Tuscany and its capital Florence provided the battleground for many a conflict through the Middle Ages. The famous Medicis held power for centuries over the abundant grape and wine center. While Chianti remains the most widely distributed, many other red and white wines.

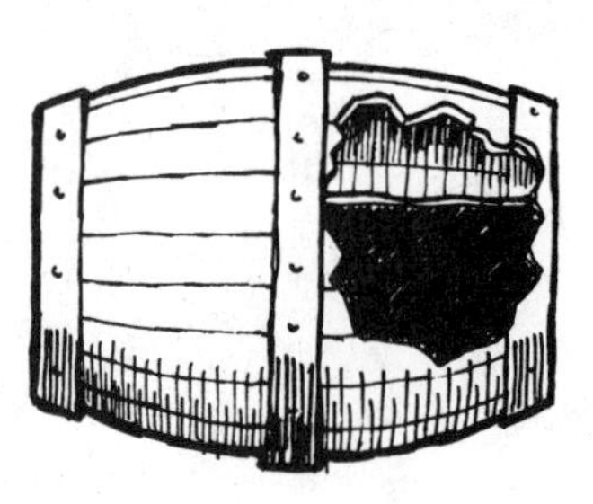

Ullage

By definition, ullage is nothing — the empty space at the head of a barrel or bottle. By common usage ullage is the amount of wine or liquor that evaporates through the sides of the aging vessel. To prevent spoilage in barrels, winemakers fill this ullage once each month!

Valpolicella

The long, narrow Valpolicella valley in Northeast Italy provides the matchless beauty of Lake Garda, and the setting for Romeo and Juliet. The star-crossed lovers undoubtedly drank the light, refreshing red wines of the area, now world varieties of Grapes, Valpolicella is the Italian Beaujolais — light, fruity, and fragrant — a wine to be enjoyed in its youth!

Venecia

The mystery and lore of Sherry is matched only by the men who make it. One of these cellar artists uses a Venecia made of whalebone with a silver cup at the tip. It is used to test the clarity of the aging wine. Thrust through the yeast cap, the cup is filled and poured into glasses without a drop spilled!

Verdelho

For a new surprise and an excellent finish to a light meal, look for a bottle of *Verdelho* in the dessert wine section. One of the four grapes used in Madeira, the Verdelho is made into a soft, medium dry wine that goes excellently with cake and ice creams.

Verdicchio

Throughout Italy, the familiar amphora-like fish bottle is known as a favorite white wine just perfect with fish. Verdicchio is produced from the grape of the same name accounting for nearly half of the Marches wine production.

Verjus

The great bulk of commonly consumed wines in France originate in the hot South. In very hot summers, the grapes mature without sufficient acid content for good flavor. Smart winemakers produce a second harvest of very highly acidic wine called verjus to balance the earlier wines.

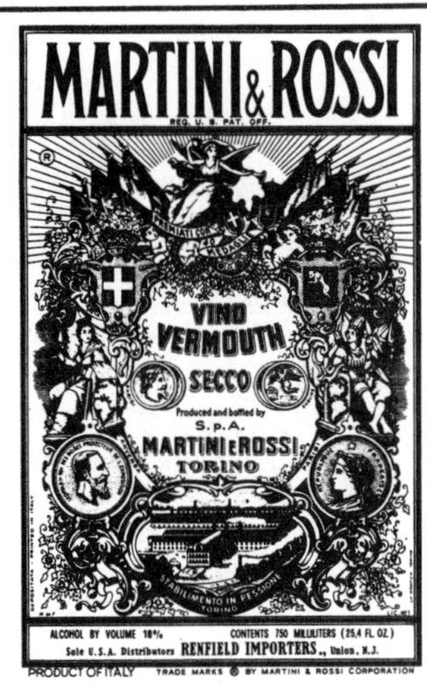

Vermouth

Vermouths are perhaps the most ancient of treated wines. They are produced by steeping or soaking wines in flavorful aromatics. Ancients flavored wines with everything from pepper to poppies. Vermouth is from the German for wormwood, a popular flavor. French type vermouth is white and dry. Italian is rich, red and bittersweet.

Vermouth Herbs

Vermouth comes from the word WERMUT which means man's strength! Ancient man believed firmly that his well-being was served by the myriad of herbs about him. This wine is flavored by as many as forty of nature's cures including allspice, cinchona, elder flowers, hyssop, marjoram, anise, cloves and orange peel. No wonder this aperitif stimulates the appetite.

Vigneron

In France, the wine grape farmer and the wine maker are both called the *vigneron.* These artisans number one and a half million out of a total forty million population. They produce twenty five percent of the entire agricultural income, and literally support a nation where every third family depends on wine vive le vigneron!

Vin Blanc Nature

Only the best cuvees are chosen for the secondary fermentation in the Champagne district of France. Those wines not selected for this exalted purpose become *vin blanc nature* or natural, white wines. Both white and slightly pink nature wines result.

Vinegar Fly

The dreaded ACETOBACTER, a microscopic bacteria, present in all wines, is familiarly called the vinegar fly. In the presence of air, it causes a secondary fermentation eliminating the ethyl alcohol making fine vinegar from fine wine. So, keep opened wines capped and in the refrigerator!

Vin Jaune

In the picturesque Jura Mountains that separate France from Switzerland, there exist strains of the unique yeast that age Spanish sherry wines. These unique *vin jaune* or yellow wines turn golden as do the sherries when covered with the yeast mold while aging in barrels.

Vin De Pays

Pronounced PAYEE, *vin de pays* is simply local wine to the Frenchman. Seldom bottled, and less seldom exported beyond the locality, these are often fine, satisfying vintages. There are forty four *vin de pays* regions, mostly in southern France.

Vineland

Leif Ericson and his hardy band touched our shores nearly one thousand years ago. To their surprise and delight, they discovered a profusion of grapevines. They dubbed our country, Vineland The Good, a name which lasted for 600 years in Icelandic literature!

Vinho Verde

Of all the oddities in the growing of grapes around the world, none matches the rigorously controlled vinho verde in Northern Portugal. Practiced for hundreds of years and now controlled by law, the grapes literally hang between dwarf oak and chestnut trees. Picked while young and high in acid, *vinho verde* produce natural effervesence in the bottle.

Vinous Wine

The term vinous can be very confusing when applied to wines. Winemakers use it specifically to describe those wines that do not possess distinctive varietal character such as a recognizable cabernet or gamay. Therefore, most of the vinous wines, such as the Thompson seedless, are used for fruit or for base bulk wines.

Vinifera Grapes

The great wine grapes of the world fall into the classification called vitis vinifera. Translated literally, that is the vine that grows wine. A warm climate species, there are over five thousand types identified with many more thousands of local names. About two hundred are grown regularly, for the wine trade.

Viticulture

Viticulture is the science — and the art — of grape growing. Grapes are consumed commercially in more forms and in greater amounts than any other fruit of the earth. As fresh fruit, as preserves, as dried raisins, in cans or as wine and brandy, grapes yield a treasury of vitamins and minerals. Vive le viticulturist!

Vitis Labrusca

The easiest way to distinguish the two great families of grapes is by the climates in which they thrive. The profusion of grape wines discovered by the Vikings in North America were of the Labrusca breed. They withstand the heavy winters and produce lovely jams, jellies and juices but lesser wines.

Vitis Vinifera

Vitis Vinifera is called the vine that grows wine. The native European vines have been cultivated at least five thousand years and propagated to all warm climates on the globe between 35 degrees south and 50 degrees north latitudv. All great wines are vinifera!

Vintage

The practice of marking the vintage year on wine labels confuses most novices. It needn't. Technically, it means no more than a harvest. The grapes were grown in that specific year. There is no relation to quality — good or bad. Vintage charts and guides provide the guesses of the experts at harvest time and are often unreliable. Trust your wine merchant or trust to luck, but don't worry too much about the year.

VDQS

Be on the lookout for this designation on imported French wines. Often you will find both quality and price in your favor. In 1949, this designation was coined — Vin Delimite de Qualite Superieure — limited wines of good quality. A step below the famous Controlee vintages, these growths are still carefully controlled and are excellent wines.

Wachstum

German wine labels must be the most complicated in Western Civilization. Very often on a Moselle wine label, there appears the word Wachstum before a surname. Think of the word as Estate Bottled as it literally means "from the property of."

Must Weight

Most people recognize that the alcohol in wine comes from the division of grape sugars into ethanol and carbon dioxide. The amount of alcohol that will be produced depends on the weight of the grape juice or must. Literally, that weight distinguishes the must from the weight of water, and it is done with a hydrometer.

Weinguteiegal Osterreigh

Every wine country, has some designation of governmental sanction for its very best quality products — such as the Black Rooster for Chianti and the Appellation Controlee in France. The Austrians use a seal which roughly translates into classified wine estate. It's your guarantee!

Wine Acidity

The most prominent characteristic of wine or any other fruit juice is acidity. Fruits and juices lacking in acidity are flat, dull and insipid. There are generally two classes and fruit acid — volatile and fixed. The volatile smells like vinegar. The fixed is actually a combination of tartaric, malic and citric acids. Every great wine has a good acid level.

Wine Bitterness

Identify bitterness with the red wines. Bitterness in wine is caused primarily by the tannin extracted from the skins during fermentation. This gentle bitter astringency is an acquired taste difficult for new wine consumers. The tannins create the taste complexities of the truly great red wines.

Wine Body

The body or viscosity of wine (as in all other fluids) is its weight or resistance to being poured. In wine a complex inter-marriage of alcohols, suspended solids, tannins and aldehydes render some heavy or full on the tongue, and other light like white wines. Aged wines tend to fuller body.

Wine Bottle

The very word bottle is a corruption of the French word for wine vessel. Though blown glass was used two thousand years earlier, at about 1680 the cork was first utilized as a wine bottle stopper and the incredible effects of wine-bottle aging achieved. Few realize that wine is the only food to grow and physically improve once bottled! A unique symphony of vintner, cork and bottle create living poetry!

Wine Boquet

Twirl the glass gently throwing the wine around the sides of the bowl. The profusion of odors that arise are called Bouquet by the wine lover. Few foods offer the complexity and range of smells — from strawberries to musty oak — from lilacs to almonds. The slow oxidation of fruit alcohols, acids and other compounds creates a sensory symphony in great aged wines!

Wine Breathing

Don't be confused or distressed about how long a wine must breathe! Wine breathing is purely and simply the oxidation or browning of the fruit juice similar to a cut apple. The glory and wonder results when this process creates enticing odors and suppleness in aged wines. As a rule reds need more breathing to reach perfection — up to an hour. Just remember, open the bottle early and pour out a bit to break the seal — and let nature take over!

Wine By-Products

It is said that the grape is the richest of all fruits because of its deep and ranging root structure. The consequence of this abundance was seen in the second world war when the by-products of grape and wine making ranged from cooking powders and salts, to shoe tanning, to potato chips, to soap making, to synthetic rubber and a host of similar commercial products.

Wine Complexity

Wine lovers nearly always advert to poetic terms to express profound reaction to superb vintages. Opaque, velvety, well-rounded, and elegant are common terms. Complexity involves the range of human sensations and it derives from the sum of all the parts from soil to aging bottle. It is a mystery! It is a symphony!

Concord Wine

The workhorse of the native American grape industry is the Concord grape. A hybrid, as are most Amrican varieties, Concord was first cultivated in 1843 and named for Concord, Massachusetts. Used widely for juice, jams and jellies, it is most noted as a creamy sweet Kosher ritual wine.

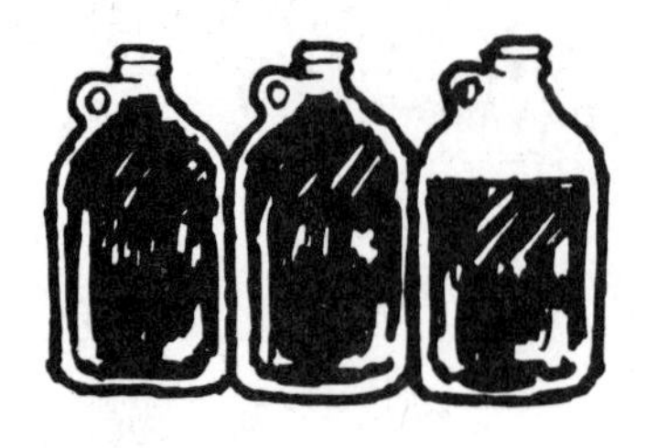

Wine Consumption

Per capita consumption of wine in our land is somewhat more than two gallons per year. It is growing steadily, particularly among young adults who drink five times the wine as their elders. By contrast, the French, Italians and Spanish exceed thirty gallons per year!

Wine Cork

Pliant, oak bark which prevents destructive air from entering bottle so wine will mature. Discovered in 17th century, corked glass replaced barrels and ancient Greek Amphora. If kept wet with wine, will last for decades.

Dessert Wines

Americans are newly discovering a treasured European practice of serving rich, full-bodied and mellow dessert wines *with desserts.* Ranging in color from the pale gold of the sherries to the tawny and ruby of the ports, the high sugar and alcohol provide appropriate accent to the meal's end.

Dry Wine

In the wine business, the word dry means no sugar. It's as simple as that. Dry wines have no detectable sugar content. Medium dry wines have a sweet overtone. Sweet dessert wines like Port or Cream sherry have up to fourteen percent sugar by volume. You either like 'em dry or you don't!

Fortified Wine

Though federal authorities have declared the term illegal, Americans still persist in describing their dessert wines as fortified. The age old process of adding clear, high proof brandy to a fermenting tank literally pickles the grapes! High fruit sugar is retained and high alcohol is assured!

Foxy Wine

Foxy wine has no relationship to the clever animal of the same name, though historically the word may have derived from native Fox grapes. Foxy simply refers to an odd, musty odor and flavor in wines caused by methyl anthranilate in indigenous grapes!

Generic Wine

Over the centuries, wines made and shipped from certain geographic areas (such as Burgundy in France) became identified with those areas. The same kinds of wines grown in other countries were then named as Burgundy, Chablis or Sherry. Usually generics are blends of a number of common grapes.

Grey Riesling

Grey Duchess or Grey Riesling is a California grand dame. Search the great wine authorities and you will seldom find this popular, soft white wine mentioned. Whatever its uncertain heritage, it is NOT a member of the popular Riesling family. Accept it for what it is ' a popular, slightly sweet California varietal.

Kosher Wine

Kosher wines by Rabbinical law are those produced pure and unmixed under supervision of a Rabbi. By general perception, they are intensely sweet, Concord grape or berry wines. While these types have popularity in America, Kosher wines used in religious festivals may be sweet, dry, table or sparkling. Local custom prevails as to type!

Hybrid Wine

The great wine grapes of the world are native to the warmer portions of the globe. In attempts to cross the hardiness of native American cold climate grapes with the finer varieties, thousands of hybrids have emerged. A few produce distinctive and pleasant wines such as the Ruby Cabernet in Cailfornia and Baco Noir, Chancellor Noir and Aurora in New York.

May Wine

During the Dark Ages, wines were flavored with nearly all available herbs both to improve the taste of bitter wines and for medicinal effects. One such blend is still found in German spring festivals. Light wine is flavored with sweet woodruff and strawberries or other fruit is added. Some May wine is bottled and exported. A light delight!

Mendoza Wine

Seven hundred miles inland from the coast of Argentina lies one of the world's most abundant and well organized wine industries. Nestled into the Andean Mountains, the province of Mendoza contains over six hundred fifty thousand acres of grapes — twice that of the United States. Fine varietals imported originally from Europe produce excellent wines.

Oxidation in Wine

You can visualize the effect of oxidation in any fruit by the browning of a cut apple. When the skin of a fruit is broken, the pulp fixes oxygen and releases hydrogen. This is perfectly natural, but equally harmful to the fruit or wine. Sulphur dioxide in minute quantities controls the oxidation of tannins, pigments and minerals. Keep your wines from exposure to air!

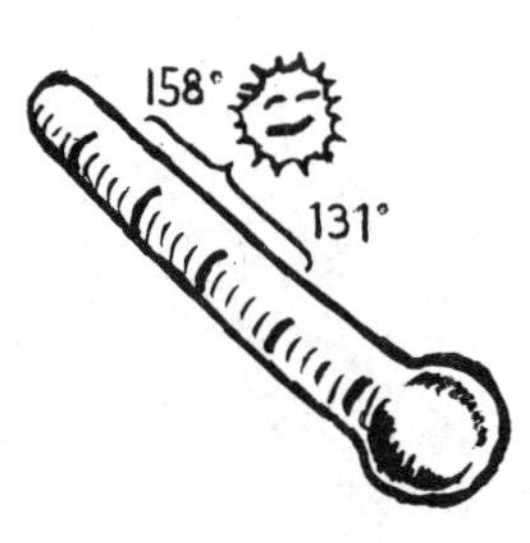

Wine Pasteurizing

Among his many contributions to man, Louis Pasteur discovered that yeast and bacteria in fluid are killed or inhibited following brief exposures to high temperatures. Great table wines are never subjected to heat, but beer and many common table and dessert wines are stabilized by pasteurizing!

pH of Wine

Literally, pH is the hydrogen ion content of the wine. Practically, it is the measure of acidity. Balanced wines have a delightful tang and tartness. Acid-deficient wines are flat and uninteresting. The best wines measure between 3 and 4 on the pH scale.

Piquant Wine

Wine writers often refer to piquancy, particularly in white wines. The dictionary declares this to be a sharply stimulating sense of taste. It is generally understood to be a sharp but pleasing level of fruit acid.

Pop Wine

The ninety percent increase in wine consumption this decade was due to prodigious guzzling by our young of sweet concoctions terms Special Natural Wines. To a nation weaned on sweet soda pop, these fusions of alcohol and fruit juices were naturals. That's why the Pops were so popular!

Wine Press

The primary objective of the winemaker is to extract the maximum juice from the grape for fermenting. The press queezes out rich liquid. From the stomping of the grapes or squeezing them through slatted barrels to the modern pneumatic steel cages, the juice is the goal.

Quick-Aged Wine

Once man discovered the unique qualities derived from aging wine, he set about to create short-cuts. Each attempt has been less than satisfactory. These range from immersion of fresh oak chips in the wine vats to literally baking the wines at 120 degrees or more. Great wines all need the gentle harmonizing of time itself!

Red Wine

Anyone who has ever bit the skin or seed of a grape can readily grasp the character as well as the process for fermenting red wines. When left in the fermenting tank, both the color and the bitterness of the skins and seeds are imparted to the wines!

Rhine Wine

In the white wine boom in the American market, nearly everything called Rhine wine is in demand. Imported Rhine wines are those which originate along the Rhine and its tributaries, from the best to the least Liebfraumilch. In America, Rhine wines are dry to medium dry, flowery pleasant but largely undistinguished vintages.

Rice Wine

The popular Saki is often called rice wine since it contains from 12-16% alcohol and is sold in a wine type bottle. This Japanese favorite since the 8th century is actually a beer! It is made by cleaning, steaming and then fermenting rice. Sakamizu means "water of prosperity".

Rosé Wine

While most wine lists carry this popular wine type as a separate category, by classification it is a red wine. It is fermented on the grape skins for a very brief period to obtain the anthocyanin pigmentation but very little of the tannins and heaviness of the reds. In terms of taste and style, the Rose'resembles the light fruitiness of the white wines!

Table Wines

Table or dinner wines quite simply are those vintages designed for consumption at the table with meals. They may be red, white or pink; are usually 12 percent in alcohol and may also range from the perfectly dry or sugarless types to those with a gentle trace of grape sugar. You be the judge. The wines you like are the proper table choices!

Wine Sediment

The sediment often found in older bottles of wine results from natural precipitation of crystals and other solids. Wineries today exercise great care in racking and filtering these tartrates, tannins and compounds before bottling . . . all of which are harmless in consumption. If found, carefully decant to another container.

Sparkling Wine

When a wine is sparkling, it contains from two to six atmospheres of carbon dioxide created by a secondary fermentation. This term covers all types — champagne is white, sparkling burgundy is red, crackling rosè is pink — but they are all sparkling wines.

Varietal Wine

A wine made from a variety of grapes. Cabernet Sauvignon is a grape variety. By law, there must be at least 75% of that varietal wine in the bottle. You'll love these select, longer aged wines.

Vintage Wine

Don't be confused! A vintage year means only that the grapes were grown in the year on the label. Otherwise, wines are blended from year to year for balance. Vintage wine may be superb or awful. Trust the brand name or ask your friendly wine merchant.

Yeast

Wine lovers the world over praise this tiny, microscropic airborne plant life called yeast. A small bucket of working yeast will ignite a twenty thousand gallon vat of grape juice. The yeast consumes the grape sugars creating alcohol and carbon dioxide. Without them, there would be no wines or brews!

Chateau d'Yquem

The first among the great rich Sauternes of Southern France without question is d'Yquem! The grapes are picked very late so that a friendly mold penetrates the skin reducing the fluid and concentrating the sugar. The resulting wine is unbelievably smooth, rich and mellow. Very expensive but truly liquid gold!

Zinfandel

The heritage of the noble red Zinfandel is shrouded in mystery. California Grapes with few exceptions are European grapes, transplanted to thrive in the ideal soil and sun. Traditionally used as a blender with other reds, Zinfandel is now emerging as a fine, fruity, light-bodied California varietal — an uniquely American wine!

The Great Craft Brewing Revolution

Quaintest thoughts—queerest fancies
Come to life and fade away.
What care I how time advances?
I am drinking ale today.
Edgar Allan Poe

The last two decades of this century have witnessed a virtual explosion in culinary adventurism. From Tex-Mex restaurants and hot chilis to hard crust German breads and the latte craze, the consumer has sought avidly for new tastes as never before in our history.

None of these dalliances has enjoyed greater – or perhaps more lasting – acceptance than the love affair with craft brews. One can find many definitions – and as many arguments – about what constitutes a craft beer. These controversies continue to rage, in and out of the courts, but they are of little concern to the newly advantaged consumer who has dozens of brew options at the corner store.

Seeded at first by the popularity of more strongly flavored import brews, Americans gravitated to the fuller, richer and often more satisfying ales and bocks which harmonized with the often piquant flavors of Thai, Greek, Mandarin, Indian and other diverse cuisines.

Micro-breweries and pub-breweries now dot the national map like dandelions on a summer lawn – at last count nearly 900 hundred of them from a base of less than 20 a scant ten years ago – each one employing new folks and contributing to local economies. It's a win/win game.

In 1982, Denver's Institute for Brewing Studies inaugurated the Great American Beer Festival. To the elation of all, 40 breweries and 700 enthusiasts attended. This year, festival planners look for over 350 breweries to bring over 1,400 brews to sate the ravenous appetites of over 25,000 paying customers.

A size perspective helps in evaluating the impact of the new-breed of brewers. One of the largest and most successful craft brewers is Boston Beer, producers of the Samuel Adams brands. With a 1995 production of around 900,000 barrels, Boston Beer is but a toddler when matched against Anheuser-Busch, the world's largest brewer at over 86 million barrels per year. The grand-daddy of American crafts, Anchor Steam, makes less than 100,000 barrels and most of the smaller outfits satisfy local market at under 20,000 barrels. But, at present, craft brewing hums along with a nearly fifty percent growth rate per year.

The highest commendation of the craft brew phenomenon has been the release of a string of new craft-style brews by mainline U. S. brewers. Several of the titans have invested in or purchased outright already established microbreweries.

Afficionados of microbrewing argue that large and/or mid-size brewers are not capable of producing full-flavored craft beers. Others criticize craft brewers who contract production with old-line brewers. Neither argument holds much water. Anyone can craft a good brew since the "craft" represents style not size.

For the consumer, these debates are frivolous. What matters is the cornucopia of new flavors and choices in the market.

Likker talks mighty laud w'en it git loose fum the jug.

Uncle Remus

Eat not to dullness. Drink not to elevation.

Benjamin Franklin

Were I to prescribe a rule for drinking, it should be . . . The first glass for myself, the second for my friends, and the third for good humor. The fourth for my enemies.

Joseph Addison

THE GERMANS BROUGHT WITH THEM A LOVE OF BEER AND STURDY BUILDINGS (University of Washington Libraries)

Man's First Big Innovation

Oh may a peer of England brew,
Livlier liquor than the muse:
And malt does more for man than Milton can;
To justify God's ways to man.
Ale, man, ale's the stuff to drink!
For fellows whom it hurts to think.
Look into the pewter pot,
To see the world, as the world's not.

A.E. Houseman

As he brews, so shall he drink.

Ben Jonson

Some say the control of fire, others gunpowder and still others the printing press represents the greatest single discovery of mortal man. Wondrous accomplishments all, but pale they do against both the antiquity and the universality of brewing. Somewhere in the deepest recesses of history, some cavewife (houses not yet being invented) noticed that some carelessly stored grains bubbled like their favored wines. The resulting fluid being found greater than the former, because of the creation of ethyl alcohol, the practice was systemized and replicated!

Some justification must be made for this claim. Beer outsells all beverages consumed by man with the single exception of coffee. Well in excess of twenty billion gallons of beer are consumed each year as compared to under eight billion gallons of wine. The drinking of beer is so fundamental that the Latin word for drinking itself, *bibere,* is the root word for beer in most other languages. Marco Polo described an ancient Chinese beer called sohshu. Archeologists have uncovered pots of brews sixteen centuries old. Beer, bread and onions formed the diet of the Egyptian commoner. Beer has been a staple in the diet of man since the earliest of times. For, like wine, beer is a fluid food. And, while the process is natural, it had to be learned by alert observers. Here are the essential ingredients they watched.

First there is the water. Lots of water. Unlike the fruit, there isn't enough water in grain to achieve fermentation or to provide the base for the fluid at consumption. Consequently, pure water sites became the natural locations for most early breweries.

Next there is the grain. All seeds can be made into beers, so the type of beer is related to the types of abundantly available regional grains. That abundance was most important since often the brewery had to fight the bakery for a limited grain supply. However, one grain in particular has been singled out through the centuries both because of its body and flavor characteristics, and also because it has within each seed more of the catalytic enzymes than are required for its own malting needs. Malting is the conversion of grain starches to grain sugars. Barley enzymes can therefore help to convert other, enzyme deficient grain starches to sugars which are used in the same brewing tank. These other grains are often called adjuncts, and they include rice and corn as well as sugars and syrups.

Finally, there are hops. Despite the common acceptance, this herb is not essential to the brewing process, but its universal use make it a mandatory ingredient. Its primary purpose is to protect the beer from deterioration, but its secondary side effect of flavor enhancement is more comonly recognized.

And, that's it. While dozens of other enhancers, stablizers, foam producers and the like are often employed in common brewing, the above three are all that's really needed. And here's how they all work.

OPEN FERMENTERS OF BYGONE DAYS LIBERALLY FOAMED WITH YEAST (Kirin Breweries)

From Malt to the Melting Pot

In malting, the seeds are germinated in large rooms just as you would germinate a seed in a flower pot in the kitchen. Warm water is applied and the seed sprouts. In this sprouting, the magical enzymes make maltose sugar out of the carbohydrates. Heat then curtails the growth, and the amount of heat determines the roast, or the final taste of the brewed malt.

Cleaned and ground, this malt is mixed with hot water to become wort. The mass is boiled to convert other starches, and finally hops are brewed into the fluid by further boiling. The cooled wort is then injected with yeast for the familiar breakdown of the sugars to alcohol and carbon dioxide. Portions of that likeable gas are reserved for injection again into the brew just before delivery to the market. Therefore, unlike most wines, brews are characterized by the effervesence of retained carbon dioxide.

The vast majority of beers have from three to five percent alcohol measured by weight, with only a few specialties rising above the six percent level. Recognize, however, that much more water is quaffed in the brew, than in wine or spirit drinks. Here's a perspective. One eleven ounce 3.5% alcohol beer, one six ounce glass of 12% alcohol wine and a one ounce shot of 40% alcohol (80 proof) brandy all contain approximately the same raw alcohol. About half an ounce. Keep this firm relationship in mind when drinking.

The individuality of beers out there in the vast melting pot of a beer market depend upon the type of malt, the extent of brewing, various types of yeast for unique fermentations, the types of other grains, hops and other additives. We've come a long way from the cavewife!

HOPS ARE BREWED INTO THE WORT IN GLEAMING COPPER BREW KETTLES (Samuel Smith Old Brewery)

Beer Adjunct

Over the years, Americans have expressed their preference for the light, pale and stable beers. These desirable flavors and character are obtained by a delicate balance of additives such as cracked corn, rice, grits, honey and even popular corn flakes!

Aguamiel

Centuries before the enterprising distillers of Jalisco developed Tequila, South Americans were benefiting from the common maguey plant. Cut bowl-like at its stem, it will produce an average of six quarts of honey-sweet aguamiel daily. A rapid fermentation of aguamiel creates native beer called Pulque.

Beer Alcohol Measured

The handy hydrometer is used to calculate the specific gravity of the beer wort before and after fermentation. Calculations then yield the percent of alcohol BY WEIGHT. This contrasts with the percentage of alcohol BY VOLUME used in most beverage alcohols.

Ale

Ale is a type of beer — a distinctive malt beverage which is brewed at higher temperature with a unique variety of yeast that rises to the top of the fermenter. Always with a pronounced hop flavor, ale often is higher in alcohol and is bitter-sweet to the taste.

Alewife

From the beginning of time, the housewife had the duty of both baking the bread and brewing the ale. It was not until commercial brewing of the late Middle Ages that the brewer took over. In Colonial America, often a widow called the Alewife was licensed for this essential task.

Yard of Ale

The tavern in ancient times as well as today was the scene of frivolity and practical joking. The yard was one of a series of "puzzle glasses" used to spill the frothy contents on an unsuspecting customer. The yard glass — literally three feet long — emerged as a popular beer glass in its own right. A yard of ale contained over three pints and required great care in the drinking!

Bamberger Rauchbier

In long gone days, the home brewer dried his brewing malt in the simplest way possible — over an open fire. The smoke imparted strong and acrid tastes similar to Scotch whiskey made from peat smoked malt. This tradition of beechwood log smoked malt is continued today in the small town of Bamberg, West Germany. For a *really different* beer, look for Bamberger Rauchbier.

Beer

Any fermented beverage that derives from malted starch may be classified as beer. Barley, corn, millet, barks and many other grains qualify. Beer was consumed so commonly in ancient times that the Latin verb *bibere* means the act of drinking. Beer was an everyday necessity.

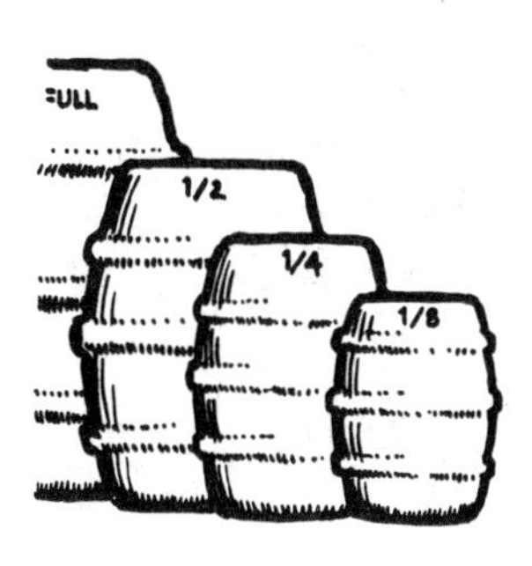

Beer Barrel

Americans are rolling out the beer barrel in numbers, but they probably would be surprised at their odd gallonages. The pitch-lined wood barrel of old has been replaced by stainless steel or aluminum. The full barrel contains exactly thirty-one gallons while the picnic or pony barrel has exactly 3.875 bubbly gallons!

Black Jack

In the Dark Ages, long before glass became affordable to the peasant, the brewing of beer was a fact of daily life. Small and medium sized drinking vessels were shaped from leather which was tanned and waxed and often decorated with baubles. Everyone had a Black Jack!

Bock Beer

Perhaps the oldest of old wives' liquor tales, handed down faithfully from one generation to the next, is that which has bock beer being brewed from the sediment of barrels cleaned in springtime. It is, rather, a special heavy and often sweeter brew usually created as a herald to approaching springtime. The name comes from Einbeck, Germany from which huge quantities of fine beer were exported in the Middle Ages.

Brew Kettle

Most people are surprised to learn that brewing is a preliminary step in making beer. The brew kettle receives malted mash called wort which is boiled furiously with an infusion of hops. The process provides new flavors and reduces the heavy solids that would cloud the beer.

Cerevisia

The words for beer in most Western nations derive from the Latin *bibere* which naturally enough means — to drink! Latin countries use *cerevisia* or *cerveza* both crediting the Roman Goddess of Grain — Ceres and the Latin word for vigor or strength which is *vis. Therefore, Latins believe they gain vigor from the grain!*

Cock and Bull Story

The telling of tall tales has never been easier than under the gentle persuasion of a friendly libation. The Cock and Bull tavern in ancient England was particularly noted as a ribald inn, a place where loose tongues weaved tales of valor and accomplishment. Hence outlandish braggadocio became identified as Cock and Bull!

Dark Beer

In dark, stout and porter, the malt or germinated barley is carmelized by roasting to produce color, "burnt" taste and fuller body. Addition of more hops produces bitterness. Porter gets a dash of licorice.

Dehydrated Beer

Believe it or not — for brewer use only — man has dehydrated even beer! Fresh beer is flash frozen creating ice crystals of about three quarters of the volume. When these snow flakes are skimmed off, you have really dry beer concentrated for ease in shipping.

Distiller's Beer

To understand nearly all liquors, you must comprehend what is termed wash or distiller's beer. The fermentation of grain mash produces this simple beer. It lacks the hop flavoring and cereal adjuncts of commercial beers. It is distilled directly into whiskey or re-distilled into vodka.

Dortmunder

Dortmund is an important, northern German town. Among other things, the brewers in Dortmund were among the first to adopt the distinctive lager style brewing which originated in Pilsen in Bohemia. These bottom fermented brews were aged in caves for weeks to achieve their light body and character.

Draught Beer

Draught (pronounced DRAFT) or tap beer is packaged in aluminum barrels at the brewery. It is the oldest and still the most popular beer, a fresh, unpasteurized brew normally consumed within a week of brewing. Have another schooner!

Festbiere

Before refrigeration, brews had to be made of great strength particularly to survive summer heat. The tradition grew to make a special beer for every major occasion — festive beers! Hence the labels had *Marzen* for March beer, *Ostern* for Easter, *Octoberfest* for harvest and so on.

Flavor in Beer

True beer lovers decry the increasing softness in American beer. Beer flavor is a complex consequence of the constituents including carbohydrates, sugars, enzymes, vitamins, minerals and principally hops (a relative of the mulberry). Unfortunately, brewers use half the hops of 1935!

Beer Foam

Universally beloved, the froth on your brew denotes quality in the product. Residue bubbles of the carbon dioxide gas created in fermentation burst to the top of the glass carrying with them a network of proteins. Abundant beer foam aids in digestion, adds piquancy by tickling the tongue and renders good taste. Here's to the head!

Ginger Beer

Discovered in the 16th century, ginger root spread quickly throughout the British Empire. Soon, flavored home beers were being made both in England and in the Colonies. Containing ginger, tartar and brown sugar, the trick with ginger beer is the bottling while still fermenting. It's a foaming delight.

Beer Grains

The abundant earth produces grain starches in many forms. Since all are fermentable following germination into sugars, brews have been a common source of beverage alcohol. By far the best of the bunch is barley, near universal in beer making. Africans use the more abundant millet and Japanese prefer rice for Sake beer. American brewers often blend corn and rice for paler color and snappier taste!

Hops Effect

Near the end of the Middle Ages an extract called Humulus Lupulus was introduced into the brewing process. Hops at that time were thought to be a veritable pharmacopia, a cure-all. It turned out that hops provided not only tart flavor but also an anti-bacterial and a preservative to the brew.

Hop Flower

The pleasing, bitter taste in beer derives from the ripened cones of the flower of the female hop vine. First used at the Monastery of St. Denis in France in 760, hops are used worldwide but in lesser degree in modern light beers.

Liquor Hydrometer

A common sight is the service station man testing anti-freeze with a glass hydrometer. The same gauged instrument measures specific gravity for both sugar content and alcohol content in liquor making. It is a gift from Ancient Greece in common use today!

Kraeusened Beer

In a system very much akin to the second fermentation in producing sparkling wines, the Kraeusening tank encloses already finished and aged beer with a dose of newly fermenting wort. The resulting carbon dioxide bubbles are bound by nature in the beer adding to the flavor and aroma.

Kulmbacher

The Erste Brewery in Northern Bavaria holds the distinction of producing the world's strongest beer — EKU 28. This malty concoction comes into being through the freezing of the brew concentrating the remaining alcohols up to 13.2 percent by volume, triple the regular American brews!

Lager Beer

A lagern in Germany is a storage area. Hence, to lager is to store or age a new brew. This period of cold aging causes a mellowing and maturing of a lively new brew. Nearly all beer you consume is lager unless it is named as ale, malt liquor, or stout or porter. Lager beer is usually light and satisfying!

Beer Life

Unlike most foods we consume from can or bottle, our beloved brew has a predictably limited life. Even the unpasteurized brew placed in the draught barrels must be consumed within thirty days. Pasteurized bottled and canned beer last no more than three months. Enjoy your brew young, fresh and bubbly!

Light Beer

In brewing, much of original barley grain starch remains in beer as dextrine, a tasteless carbohydrate. By eliminating dextrine, beer calories drop from about 136 to about 90 per bottle. VIOLA, LIGHT CALORIE BEER!

Liberty Tree

In Colonial days, the tavern was the community center, the post-office, the government rooms as well as the social hall. Helping to plot the Revolution, a band of wealthy men met as a secret society called The Sons of Liberty. For protection, the gathered in a tree house in what they called The Liberty Tree outside of Montagne's Tavern in New York City.

Malted Grain

Malting is one of the stages in the life cycle of grain which is caused by the application of heat and moisture. The grains produce new shoots by germinating. The grain starches are transformed into maltose, a sugar, which can be yeast fermented producing beer. Malting is a must to produce beer and hard liquor.

Malt Liquor

All brew is composed of malt, hops and water. But malt liquor has the considrable advantage of up to 6.5% alcohol by weight as contrasted to the 4% or less alcohol in regular beers. In addition, hotter fermentations yield lighter body and often sweeter tastes.

Near Beer

It took that determined woman Carrie Nation and her familier axe to reduce the brew of ancient times to its cereal level. During prohibition, the alcohol was distilled or cooked out of perfectly good beer reducing it to liquid breakfast food — this called Near Beer!

Pasteurizing

Canned and bottled brew is stablized much as milk by the process of pasteurization. Once bottled, it is shuttled slowly through a chamber in which heat is gradually applied and removed. The active yeast and bacteria alike are destroyed.

Pilsner

Pilsoner originated in the Bohemian town of Pilsen in 1292. A particular strain of hops from that area yields a tart, pleasant aroma and taste, and the local yeast produces a light brew. Other light brews around the world have borrowed the name but never matched the original!

Porter

The English enjoy their beers sweet and warm. Porter, named for the waiters who deliver it, is a top-fermenting ale. It is dark brown from the roasted malt used in brewing and has a heavy, pleasing foam with just a touch of hops. Three cheers for the Porters!

P's and Q's

In the 1600's in Colonial America, the tavern keeper had a difficult job. By law he had to provide beer and cider to his guests but he was fined if they got drunk. So, he kept track by marking down a P for a pint and a Q for each quart sold to a patron. Minding his P's & Q's.

Pub

A Pub is a Public House. In England and pioneer America, the Public House was an integral unit of society. Serving often as post office, courtroom, inn, restaurant and barter house as well as social center. Many of the historic meetings leading to our revolution and freedom were held in Pubs!

Pulque

Manana is manageable to the Mexican through the magic of pulque — his native beer. The productive Maguey cactus will yield up to twelve gallons a day of sweet sap which is fermented in leather to a six percent brew. The same brew distilled is known as Tequila!

Rienheits-gebot

One consequence of the incessant warfare of medieval Europe was the need for money. In 1516 Wilhelm IV, Duke of Bavaria, sought to purify beer to attract more customers — and more tax dollars. To this day, the Rienheitsgebot assures Bavarian brews add nothing to the pure barleymalts, hops and water.

Sidra

One of the most ancient of alcoholic beverages is apple cider. The word *sidra* is Spanish for cider. Both words derive from the Hebrew *shekhar,* found often in the Bible referring to strong drink. Cider and sidra are the ferments of fresh apple juice.

Stadt Huys

Governor Wilhelm Kleft ruled pioneer New York City in 1642. Recognizing the need for both order and recreation, he built a tavern which soon became known as Stadt Huys — City Hall — since it was the center of the affairs of state.

Steam Beer

The only American firm now producing steam beer is Anchor Brewers of San Francisco. The *steam* merely refers to the heavier than usual carbonation induced in the aging process designed to preserve the beer longer without refrigeration. This firm uses only pure barley malt and makes a number of specialty beers.

Bucket of Suds

Not so many years ago, the majority of beer sold came from wooden barrels as draught beer. It was necessary to send a container to the corner tavern to get beer. A practice grew of larding the sides of the pail to prevent the precious cargo from foaming. Hence, the bucket still had its *suds.*

Stout

Every tourist in England can attest to the pungent aroma and bittersweet taste of the country's popular stout brew. Slightly higher in alcohol than lager beer, stout gets its pleasing taste from extra hops and distinctive malt.

Tied House

A tied house saloon was one under the contract or the virtual control of a brewery. The venerable old tavern, laden with political and historical traditions descended to its lowest ebb under this system now outlawed in the United States.

Wassail

At different times, the word *wassail* has been used to describe a festival, a bowl and a toast. The last is most correct since the word derives from the Anglo-Saxon *wes hal* meaning to be in good health. Many ingredients are found in *wassail* recipes.

Weiss Beer

A popular variation of the ever popular brew in Germany is Weissbrau. Literally, the word means white and the lightness comes from using wheat as the grain instead of barley. High in carbon dioxide, it foams liberally and happily in the glass.

New Brew Language

If barley be wanting to
make into malt,
We must be content and
think it no fault.
For we can make liquor to
sweeten our lips,
Of pumpkins, of parsnips,
of walnut-tree chips.

Old song

The styles of brewing are many and the variations within those styles are daunting, if not bewildering. For the enthusiastic novice, it is sufficient to recognize first the classic brewing modes – top fermenting and bottom fermenting. For ales, the yeast cells operate in wild confusion atop the wort. For lagers, bottom fermenting yeasts work deep within the brew worts in the same manner as wine fermentations.

With kudos to Charles Finkel's Merchant du Vin, brew importer and microbrewer extraordinaire, here is a listing of the classic brewing styles with brief descriptions of what makes each distinctive.

TOP FERMENTED BEERS

PALE ALE: The classic British beer is truly pale in color, though often darker than the popular American lagers. It tends to copper in color and has a clear, assertive flavor.
BROWN ALE: Traditional in the Northeast of England, it is rich, dry and often has a hint of honey. Slightly reddish, it is balanced and smooth on the palate.
PORTER: Another classic ale, porter introduces chocolate hints from its roasted malts. A full bodied, mellow choice.
STOUT: Stouts tend to be higher in alcohol content and quite dark in color. They are hearty and tend to molasses-like flavors.
DUBLIN STOUT: An extremely bitter, extra dark beer – the espresso of beer.
OATMEAL STOUT: This rich, dark, smooth beer is produced with some oatmeal malt.
MILK STOUT: True to its name, this beer has lactic acid tones, is low in alcohol and medium sweet in taste.
IMPERIAL STOUT: Also known as Russian stout, this is a very strong, quite dark and fruity beer.
SCOTCH ALE: Scotland is noted for strong, medium dark, full-bodied ales.
ALT: The German word for ale, alts range in color from light to dark depending upon where in Germany they are made.
WHEAT BEER: The only exception to pure barely malts in Germany is wheat beer which uses some wheat malt. They are light and fruity (particularly American micros) or dark (dunkel in Germany) bocks.
KOLSCH: This is a light, delicate ale made in Cologne, Germany.
TRAPPIST: Trappist ales are produced in monasteries in Belgium, Holland and Germany. While they have a wide range of tastes, many are bottle-conditioned and can improve from long aging like wines.
ABBEY ALE: Another powerful, monastic style beer, often dark and heady.
COPPER ALE: Aged like wine in oak casks, the beer takes on a brilliant copper hue and winey taste. Primarily from Belgium.
GUEUZE LAMBIC: Malted barley and wheat are spontaneously fermented by native yeasts imparting unique wine flavors to this Belgian specialty.

FARO LAMBIC: This ale is medium dry, golden in hue and quite sweet due to an infusion of candy sugar —the Vouvray of brews.
KRIEK LAMBIC: This spontaneously fermented ale is flavored with black cherries.
FRAMBOISE LAMBIC: Fresh Belgian raspberries are added to the lambic base creating a light, fruit-fragrant brew.

BOTTOM FERMENTED BREWS

LAGER: Since all bottom-fermented beer is lagered or aged for varying periods before sale, this is the overall term applied to this style of brewing.
PILSNER: Pilsner takes its name from the Czechoslovakian city where it originated in 1842. It is one of the best known styles, a highly hopped, fresh, light bodied refreshing brew —the chablis of brewing.
EXPORT: This term means different things in different places. In Germany, it is synonymous with Dortmunder beers which were shipped and enjoyed over the Continent. As a class, they tend to be slightly stronger in alcohol content than Pilsners but are not highly hopped like ales. In the U.S., Export beers are often called "malt liquors."
DORTMUNDER: "Dortmund" is tantamount to "Export" but the beer must come from this city which is Germany's largest beer shipper.
DARK BEER: Beer labeled "dark" is most often a Munchener style, even though most Munich beers today are Pilsner or Export. The dark colors come from a high percentage of roasted malt which imparts a full, rich coffee-like color and assertive taste.
BIERE DE PARIS: Paris was once one of Europe's major brewers. This style is copper-colored, like an ale, but the brew often is high in alcohol with strong malty flavors.
BOCK: Bock derives from the German word for a male goat which is shown on bock labels. Brews of this type were traditionally made stronger and darker to withstand the rigors of hot summers without refrigeration. Some breweries now produce bocks throughout the year. It is a powerful, chocolate-dark brew with a noticeably high alcohol content.
DOPPLEBOCK: Extra dark and extra strong, "double" bock is a specialty of Bavaria.
SMOKED BEER: The smoke refers to a dark, Bavarian beer produced only in and around the city of Bamberg. Its unique color and smoky flavors derive from drying the malt over moist beech-wood logs in the manner of Scotch whisky.
VIENNA BEER: Although once one of the major brewing capitols of the world, Vienna on a label now refers primarily to a copper-colored, dark beer made from roasted barley malts.
STEAM BEER: This is a sienna colored remnant of California's Gold Rush. It is a mellow, dark, full-bodied lager.
HOLIDAY BEER: A tradition exists in many countries to produce special brews to be consumed at Christmas, Easter and on other important holidays. Holiday beers generally are of higher alcohol content and slightly darker than regular lagers. Often now they are flavored with various fruit essences.

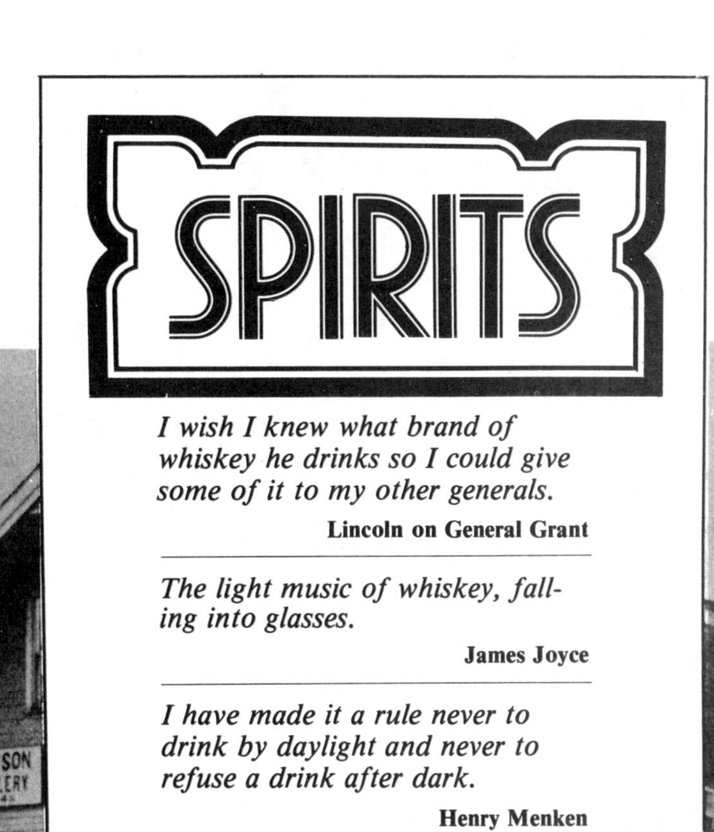

SPIRITS

I wish I knew what brand of whiskey he drinks so I could give some of it to my other generals.

Lincoln on General Grant

The light music of whiskey, falling into glasses.

James Joyce

I have made it a rule never to drink by daylight and never to refuse a drink after dark.

Henry Menken

PROHIBITION INCREASED DRINKING AS MEN CREATED INGENIOUS STILLS (The Seattle Times)

Make Mine Whiskey, Please

Glenlivet it has castles three
Drumin, Blairfindy, and Deskie;
And also one distillery,
More famous than the castles three.

Anonymous

Humanity I love you because when you're hard up, you will pawn your intelligence to buy a drink.

e. e. cummings

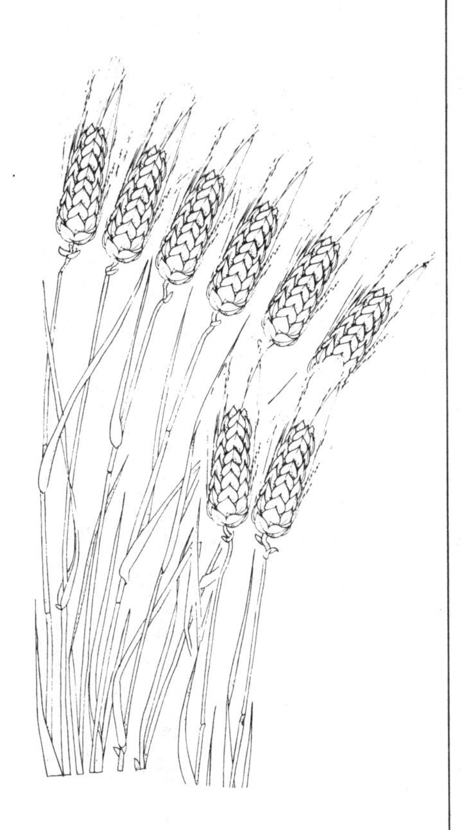

The leading whiskey producing nations of the world are the United States, Canada, Scotland and Ireland. The United States alone consumes a phenomenal total of over 220,000 millions of whiskey (whisky) gallons! Divide that up, and it amounts to over 15 bottles per year per person.

These large figures help to focus on the place that whiskey has held traditionally among the American alcohol consuming public, a leadership now undergoing considerable change. The movements to light and white, to wine and to the lighter rums, tequilas and vodkas has displaced this phenomenal and persistent penchant for heavy, dark spirits.

The Spirituous World

Don't be misled. Any form of ethyl alcohol will intoxicate. And every form has been used to that end since man first stumbled upon the product of natural fermentations. But, the goods and the evils of alcohol consumption both were enormously enliven-when Middle Age's man applied an ancient technique of heat purification to wine and beer. The spirit or essence of the fermented juice was distilled into an enormously more potent beverage.

Around the year 1120, chemists in Salerno, Italy combined the two different chemical processes, one natural and the other applied. The alcohol in natural fermentation of yeast of sugars for wines, or malted starches for brews, was wedded to a well developed technique used to extract many cooking and commercial oils, flavoring essences and cosmetics from mashed herbs and fluids.

Distillation is based upon the fact that everything has a melting point, and differing portions of every compound melt at different heats. A prime example is the ages old practice of purifying saline water through the release of the water from the salt in the form of steam. The Chaldeans and Egyptians first utilized rudimentary stills to obtain commercial and artistic products. Eight hundred years after the birth of Christ, an Arabian alchemist named Gerber set forth the following dictim:

> *Distillation is the raising of aqueous vapor in any vessel . . . Sometimes it is performed by fire, sometimes without it . . . The object of distillation is to free liquors from dregs and to preserve them fresh, since everything distilled possesses a greater purity.*

More to our point, alcohol vaporizes at about 176 F, a much lower temperature than the water and grape solids that form the base of the wine. Water requires 212 F degrees to boil. Hence, the heat applied to wine will first release the alcohol as steam long before the water.

The Italian chemists exulted in a new *medicine,* the *spirit* of wine which was subsequently applied to a gaggle of man's ills through eight centuries, and is prescribed yet today for many a physical ailment. Just look at the name universally applied to the stuff. Raymond Lully first called it *eau de vie,* or water of life, and that exalted cognomen is common in all languages. Although one scholar attributes the word alcohol to ancient Sanskrit for poison, Lully described the general acceptance of alcohol as; "An emanation of the Divinity, an element, newly revealed to man but hidden from Antiquity, because the human race was then too young to need this beverage destined to revive the energies of modern decrepitude."

The Proof's In The Still

A still is simply a mechanical device of varying sizes and proportions designed to separate that ethyl alcohol from the wine at various chemical concentrations. The simplest of stills can be made by placing a pot on a kitchen stove coupled with some method of channeling the steam and cooling it so that the alcohol once again becomes a fluid. At the most complex level, huge continuous stills with vaulting cylinders of several stories in height are capable of heating thousands of gallons of wine or beer per hour, fractioning the resulting steam into dozens of chemical components and the alcohol at dozens of intensities.

Two concepts are required to understand modern application of this ancient technique. The first is the of chemical fractioning or division. Think of the various levels of petroleum — from turgid motor oil, to heavy kerosine, to light gasoline and you visualize what happens as the heat separates different components from that dark fluid sucked from the earth. Chemists use the word congener as an umbrella term to encompass all the many old and new chemicals created in this intense heat treatment of wine and beer.

Naturally, then, the taste of any spirit is determined by the concentration of its congeners — its chemical properties that survive the heat. This can be easily recognized by sniffing a vodka next to a cognac. The former has had all of the chemicals except the alcohol itself removed by intensive distilling. The latter has a pungency from those chemicals that can be perceived at ten paces! Congeners — aldehydes, fusel oils, esters, and the like — create the tastes and the smells in distilled spirits.

The second concept is man made confusion. It is called the *proof*. Originally, the concept was valid. A merchant in the Middle Ages had to prove there was sufficient alcohol in the fluid he was selling, and he did so often by flaming it. Nowadays, proof doesn't prove or approve, it is only a convenient mechanism of governments to extract taxes.

The easiest way to solve the riddle is to remember that in the United States, by governmental fiat, the proof registers exactly double the raw alcohol content. All commercial spirits must be cut by purified water to be potable. Raw spirits — everclear — would burn the mouth that surrounded it. A hun-proof bourbon contains fifty percent alcohol and fifty percent distilled water in the bottle. An eighty proof brandy contains forty percent ethyl alcohol and sixty percent water. A twenty eight proof cordial — and there are many of them — contains fourteen percent alcohol. Most of us choose our spirits because of their taste, their mixability, or their use, and never bother to notice the small print!

Compounding — A Combination of Tastes

One by one through the centuries, the flora that covers the globe has been tested in the diet of man and animal alike. The farmers know that some tasteful weeds will kill his livestock. The livestock avoid others through the process of experience. The chemical components in many rare and common plants create very certain physical effects — from purgatives to hallucinogenics. Most of these plants and herbs have been discarded from common consumption, and modern medicine has further reduced their number in therapy. However, as flavoring agents, these condiments happily survive.

Many an ancient wine *had* to be treated with condiments to make it drinkable. Liqueurs or cordials were *based* upon a mixture of the new alcoholic spirits and favorite tastes from licorice to loganberry. Aperitif wines — most notably vemouth — originate from the steeping of dozens of favorite herbs in high alcohol wines. Naturally enough, these common home concoctions drifted into commercial production.

The alcohol beverage field is replete with thousands and thousands of regional concoctions which combine,, along the production line, fermented and distilled fluids. These are further refined by the soaking of herbs and flavorings as in tea, the pumping through of others as in coffee, the heating of yet others as in sherry and madeira wines, and the redistillation of many of the above in popular liqueurs.

Compounds, in wines and spirits, result from fads or favorite flavorings. They now result from commercial application of proven home recipes. As Herrick put it so aptly in *Hesperides:* "Next crowne the bowl full with gentle lamb's wool; Add sugar, nutmeg, and ginger, with store of ale too; and this you must due to make the wassaile a swinger."

NEITHER SLEET NOR SNOW COULD KEEP THEM FROM THEIR APPOINTED TASK *(Hiram Walker, Inc.)*

Scotch, Irish and American Whiskies

I should be deficient in gratitude
to worthy Sir John Barleycorn if I had
not bestowed a few words on him who
has so often been a friend of the wet
and the weary, who has smoothed the rude
path over the mountains, and levelled the
boistrous waves of the Western Ocean.

John Macculloch

Since the fifteenth century, the industrious Scots have produced their single malt barley spirits in flavorful, small pot stills. Since the middle of the last century, corn spirits have been blended into the pot product and Scotch Whisky has played a role wherever His Majesty's ships sailed. Since post-Colonial times, American corn and rye spirits, and eventually Bourbon, have played a similar role in the U.S. Since supplying the whisky for General Washington's troops in the Revolutionary War, Canadians have produced their lighter, mixed grain whisky, their most popular export to this day.

Vast differences in production dictate the widely differing tastes of whiskies. The peat smoke marks Scotch without doubt; triple distilling softens the silky Irish blends; a wide range of styles and tastes result from heavy charred oak aging in Bourbons, and the light to heavier American blends, with the generally lighter Canadian blends.

Since great ranges of character and style are found within the whiskey category, one must search deliberately and carefully to find the right bottle. It's there!

Cognac, Brandy and White Fruit Spirits The Water of Life

Claret's the drink for boys,
Port for men.
But he who aspires to be a hero,
Must drink brandy.

Samuel Johnson

What more could be asked of a liquor, than that it makes the hero and maintains the youth! Indeed, through five centuries, brandy has maintained a pre-eminent position among the vast liquor cabinets of the world. Perhaps it is a reflection of the esteem for the wines from which it rises.

Brandies are produced wherever wines are vinted. This premier of all drinking spirits is also employed as the additional liquor needed to fortify the many hundreds of ports, sherries, vermouths, angelicas, madeiras, moscatos and other dessert wines.

Drinking brandies are distilled from fresh, ripe and rather tart grapes that lend a piquancy to the finished distillate. Various methods of production, from the small and orderly cognac stills in Southern France to the massive continuous stills of Southern California, dictate the style of the spirit. Generally, but not always, brandy is rectified by a sweet material such as sweet sherry wine. Brandies are easily sipped as traditional after dinner drinks. However, in recent years, the lighter California brandies have emerged as light but characterful cocktail mixers in contrast to the heavier traditional spirits.

Try this water of life, with the spirit of youth!

Gin — Dutch Courage

Gin: A modern nickname for the liquor called "genevra" or "genevre;" because when beggars are drunk, they are as great as kings.

Bailey's Dictionery (1720)

Dr. Sylvius produced gin as a medicine at the University of Leyden in Holland over three hundred years ago. His intent to found a better, more tasteful diuretic may well have been achieved. Along the way, he created the liquor which held the British Empire in sway, if not in bondage for those centuries.

British soldiers stationed on the continent took this new spirit to heart, and to England and dubbed it gin. Easier to pronounce than the French name for the juniper berry, its main additive. Other additives used today in making gin include caraway, coriander seeds, bitter almond, cinnamon, citrus peels, fennel, cassia bark, licorice, anise and cardamon.

Gin remains one of the most inexpensive of liquors in that it is ready to consume the moment it is redistilled or compounded with this host of flavoring agents. About five dollars of botanicals are needed for one hundred gallons of gin. While sold unaged, remarkable taste differences emerge from the base spirits used. Dutch gins remind one of bourbons; American gins reek juniper.

Take your pick, all gins have unique and interesting character.

THE COGNAC STYLE COPPER POT STILLS BECAME THE STANDARD WORLDWIDE (Asbach Uralt)

Cordials and Bitters

De quibus est res, ut rata fiat,
publicum fecimus instrumentum.
We have executed a public document concerning the matters which the transaction deals with, so that it may be confirmed.

Ratafia of the Middle Ages

A supposed drug or essence capable of indefinitely prolonging life.

Shorter Oxford Dictionary

No other commercial spirit can claim the patrimony of cordials and bitters. First, both were introduced for purely medicinal purposes, to alter the well being of users. Second, liqueurs in the form of ratafia were actually required to complete international diplomatic concords.

No other commercial spirits have such grandiose and disparate source materials. Nearly everything that tastes or smells well in its own right is utilized in the production of liqueurs. Fruits, seeds, herbs, peels, dairy products, honey — you name something of unusual and sharp character and it is involved in some liqueur.

No other commercial spirit involves so many diverse methods in production. Sure, gin is compounded of many macerated herbs. Liqueurs quite often involve maceration, percolation, distillation, and rectifying, all over the widest base of differing spirits in the universe.

No other commercial spirit enjoys so wide a range of prices as liqueurs. Some of common origin like creme de menthe fall at the bottom of the price lists. Others, of mysterious and complex, carefully guarded recipes, rise to the top rungs of the price ladder.

No other commercial spirit has so many diverse types as to satisfy the most arcane of serving needs. The right cordial brings warm smiles from your guests, and satisfaction the evening through. A lifetime of cordial distraction awaits your palate.

THE MONKS AT CHARTREUSE TEND THEIR TANKS AND STILLS WITH CARE (Chartreuse Liqueurs)

Yo Ho Ho and
A Bottle of Rum
The Truly American Spirit

Wits may laugh at our fondness for molasses, and we ought to join in the laugh with good humor. I know not why we should blush to confess that molasses was an essential ingredient in American independence. Many great events have proceeded from much smaller causes.

John Adams

While thoughts of American independence were yet to be imagined when rum was born, this distillate of Carribean sugar cane was truly destined to be an instrumental spirit in the break with England. While tea became the symbol used by prudent historians, it was truly heated molasses that was decisive in the Revolution.

Rum became the ballast for seafaring ships bound back to England as well as the payment for slaves from the African continent. It became, before the emigration of the Scotch-Irish distillers, the primary alcoholic beverage of the colonies. Actually, centures before, rum had been made into the many araks of the Mediterranean basin.

is made, rum can be both light and heavy, pure white and deep mahogany, completely dry and markedly sweet. As with wine, the natural cane sugar is fermented, and the resulting beer distilled in a variety of ways to make everything from the pungent pot still types to the light Puerto Rican varieties. The most popular brand in the American market, Bacardi, represents the delicate, fragrant end of that spectrum. Deep and full bodied Jamaican rums represent the other.

THE CONTROL BOARD OF A MODERN CONTINUOUS STILL DWARFS ITS WORKERS (The Christian Brothers)

The Vodka Swirl

When thy neighbor's cheek begins to flush, leave off drinking.

Russian Proverb

It is the Russian's joy to drink; we can not do without it.

The Primary Chronicle

The One Truly Russian Discovery

Little water truly originated, at least by name, in Russia. Even then, it must be pointed out that the clear, white grain spirits were produced also from historic times in Poland, Latvia, Lithuania, Estonia and all of the other neighboring states. But, a Russian perfected the vodka charcoal filtering process, and a Tsar favored the Smirnoff brand which later emigrated with its owner to the U.S. So, vodka truly can be called Russian.

The schnapps and akvavits of northern Germany and Scandinavia also bear great resemblence to these often flavored, continental white vodkas. But it took the United States government to create the definitive vodka, one that by law must have no taste or character, one that must be thoroughly charcoaled to remove any vestige of congeneric character.

Thus American vodka is the quintessential distilled spirit. Just the alcohol and the purified water. That's all. The purest of spirits.

VODKA AND NEUTRAL SPIRITS PRODUCED ON A MASSIVE SCALE *(Grain Processing Company)*

The Tequila Sunrise

There is a superior variety of mescal *produced near Guadalajara, and called after the village in which it is made 'Tequila' (pronounced Tekela). This costs more and is sent to the city of Mexico and elsewhere, as something very choice to present to one's friends. I took one drink of it under the supposition that it was anisette, or some other light liqueur, swallowing about one ounce, druggists measure, before I smelled the burning flesh as the lightning descended my throat.*

Col. Albert S. Evans

A Meteor on the Spirit Horizon

While Tequila has always been the favorite of the genteel in its native habitat, the very aromatic and mixable white spirit is consumed by the young of America. An extremely popular road trip by the Rolling Stones rock music group established the sticky sweet Tequila Sunrise, and the Margarita, a salt rimmed blend featuring lime juice and triple sec. Soon all the traditional mixers, the Manhattan, the Bloody Mary and the lot found new life with Tequila as a base. Sales skyrocketed, and the growing popularity of the Mexican cuisine has added new fuel to its rockets.

Produced from a single cactus, the Tequilana Weber, Tequila remains the product of a single geographic area in the manner of French cognac. Other cactus spirits made in Mexico of much harsher style are known as Mescal.

The heart of the plant, a large bulb of 20 pounds or more contains up to 20 percent sugar. This highly fermentable juice is rolled, cooked and mashed apart from the fiber, to be fermented and then distilled in small pot stills. Since Tequila is the most aromatic of all popular spirits, only one half of each final mash must originate from the blue tequila plant, the remainder being molasses. Not to fear, as tequila remains a most distinctive drink.

COOKED, ROLLED, BREWED AND DISTILLED, THESE HEARTS YIELD TEQUILA (Assoc. of Tequila Producers)

Absinthe

In the naughty Paris of 1890, the Cocktail hour was called *l'heure verte* or the green hour in honor of Absinthe. The liqueur made from heavy infusions of wormwood (artemesia absinthium) anise, spinach nettles and herbs is now banned since it was feared to drive people mad. Pernod with heavy anise flavor is its successor!

Advocaat

A strict construction of the word would mean "water of the famished." This is but one of the many variations of the original theme of aqua vitae or water of life. The Spanish speaking call many liquors by this name whether from grain, grape or cane sugar.

Aguardiente

A strict construction of the word "water of the famished." This is but one of the many variations of the original theme of aqua vitae or water of life. The Spanish call many liquors by this name whether from grain, grape or cane sugar. sugar.

Beverage Alcohol

Wine, beer and honey wine called mead have been consumed in nearly all countries and through all times. Refinements of fermenting and distilling have created a bewildering array of potables which combine ethyl alcohol with every form of pleasant flavoring. Any liquid with more than one half a pecent of ethyl alcohol is termed a beverage alcohol and thus subject to federal taxes.

Does Alcohol Raise Body Temperature?

To the surprise and dismay of many, alcoholic drinks actually lower body temperatures. A person feels warmer as heat escapes through the skin pores. In fact, rum, popular in warm climates, cools more than ice water!

Denatured Alcohol

Ethyl alcohol is denatured by adding nauseating, poisonous substances such as formaldehyde, kerosene, gasoline, shellac and pine tar. It is then a jack-of-all-trades used in everything from shampoo to embalming fluid.

Wood Alcohol

As contrasted with what we drink, the denatured type is composed of lethal methyl alcohol. Originally fermented from wood, it is made today of carbon monoxide and hydrogen. It is used in commercial products such as shellac and solvents. Blindness and death can result from human consumption. Beware!

Alembic

The alembic is the pot still used to make cognac in Southern France. Over four thousand of these simple devices are in use. They consist of a boiler, a head for the wine, a copper coil condenser and the receiving barrel. The rich, flavorful pungency of cognac comes from these simple country stills.

Al Kohl

AL KOHL, known to us as alcohol, is attributed to an Arabian alchemist in the year 800 who developed distilling from native brews. Since the magic was accomplished by vaporizing in the same manner as a popular cosmetic eye paint called KOHL, he dubbed it Al Kohl or like kohl.

Amaretto

The newly popular cocktail — THE GODFATHER — owes its piquant, smooth taste to a 56 proof liqueur made from apricot pulp and kernels. Called Amaretto, it has been appreciated for over 400 years in its native Italy. Just mix it with scotch or bourbon. Atsa Vera nize!

Anisette

Hippocrates loved his anisum. The Frenchman and Spaniard of today treasure their soothing after dinner drinks made from the common pimpinella anisum and a dozen or so other milder herbs and seeds. Licorice-like anisette is very sweet, low in alcohol and provides a nice finish to a meal.

Anisone

Perhaps the most popular taste in liqueurs is the exquisite, tangy-sweet anise seed. A popular flavor also in breads and puddings, anise is the base for Anisette, one of the sweetest cordials produced around the world. The Italian version called Anisone is typically higher in alcohol and lower in sugar. Bella, Bellisimo!

Aquavit

Aquavit, akvavit, akevit in Scandinavia or Schnapps in Germany all are in a family of pure, white native spirits quite often distilled from potatoes. In both sweet and dry fiery versions, aquavit is commonly flavored with carraway seed and cummin. Try it, like the Swedes, chilled with smorgasbord!

Aqua Vitae

The Spanish alchemist Arnold of Vila Nova first ascribed medicinal qualities to distilled spirits around 1260. He called them Water Of Life and grandly praised their restorative powers. In other languages from Gaelic to French the theme recurred — Eau de vie, Uisege Baugh — waters of a better life!

How Old are Aperitifs?

Aperitifs date from most ancient times. Greek herbalists were fond of soaking their ritual concoctions in wines to make them more palatable — and probably more effective! Fruits, flavoring agents, seeds, flowers and herbs were used. Vermouth became the first commercial aperitif in the late 18th century. Ranging from dry to semi-sweet, aperitifs sharpen the appetite and therefore are correctly used before the meal.

Armagnac

The grape brandy produced in the district of Gers in Southern France lays exclusive claim to the name Armagnac. It is said to possess a drier, harder taste than Cognac derived from the hard, black oak of Gascony in which is it aged.

Arrack

One of the common terms for liquor in Asia is arrack, often spelled araka, arraki, arak or raki. From Greece through the Middle East, it encompasses liquors made from everything from palm sap to cane sugar rum. Enjoy it on your tour with boiled eggs and cheese!

Asbach Uralt

While most German brandies are of inferior quality, Asbach Uralt is treasured throughout the western world. The key to quality in this Rudesheim distillery is the wine which is imported from the Cognac and Armagnac regions of France. Light, mellow German brandy from French wines is aged in French Limousin wood. A cooperative delight!

D'Alpe

Literally, Fior De'Alpe means the flower of the Alps in the liquor cabinet. It means a rich, heavy liqueur reminiscent of Chartreuse and often of over 100 proof potency. Always containing some northern Italian flowers and herbs, the dominant tastes are vanilla and anise!

Abricotine

Second only to cherries, the luscious apricot is the favorite source for fruit liqueurs. Grown all over the Mediterranean basin, the apricot is ideal for a tangy, semi-sweet after dinner liqueur such as *Abricotine,* produced in France by Garnier since 1959.

Batavia Arak

One of the delights of the rum trade in Batavia Arak made from molasses in Java, East Indies. A special wild yeast and local rice are added to the fermenting tubs. The rum is aged in Java four years, then shipped to Holland from more aging and bottling. A light, quaint, delightful rum!

Benedictine, D.O.M.

Benedictine is a world famous, richly sweet plant liqueur. First made in 1510 as a medicinal nostrum by monks, it utilizes many seed and herbs with cognac as the liquor. D.O.M. on the label means TO GOD, MOST GOOD, MOST GREAT.

Bitters

Without doubt, bitters are the least recognized of alcoholic beverages. A type of cordial, bitters are now used primarily to flavor mixed drinks, though they once were stomach balms. Highly aromatic seeds, barks or roots are soaked in spirits to release the unique flavors found in your favorite cocktail.

Bootlegger

Far from the romantic image, a true bootlegger was a small, pint-sized flask in common use during the stage coach era. The small bottle could be filled at each tavern stop and conveniently carried in the high boots of the time.

Bourbon

Bourbon is a distinctive robust beverage alcohol first distilled by Rev. Elijah Craig in Bourbon County, Kentucky. Bourbon must be distilled from a mash of 51 percent or more of corn and it cannot be taken above 160 proof to ensure a strong congeneric flavor. Aging in new charred oak barrels lends another important taste to America's unique drink!

Brandy

Brandy is liquor from distilling of wine or fermented fruit mash. Wine brandy is aged in wood and may be savored straight or mixed in any cocktail. Cognac is French wine brandy from Charente-Maritimes Provinces.

Fruit Flavored Brandy

In truth, *Flavored Brandy* is a misnomer but it is also a pleasant cordial prepared in many a kitchen. Whether real grape brandy or vodka is employed as the spirit base, it is made by soaking the fruit mash until the aroma and taste transfer to the spirit. There is no distillation as in true brandy.

Napoleon Brandy

Don't be confused! If someone offers you a nineteenth century Napoleon Brandy, watch your purse. No liquor ages once bottled except wine. However some fine contemporary Napoleon labeled cognacs are produced that see up to twenty years aging in wood before bottling. Buy the latter with confidence and expectation. Shun the former!

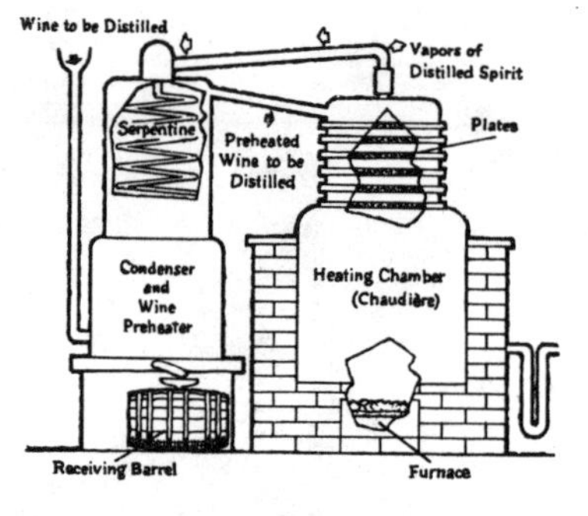

Pot Still Brandy

Blindfolded, anyone can easily pick the pungent bouquet and the commanding tastes of European brandy and cognac. The ancient pot still is the cause of the distinction in the spirit. Simplicity itself, the all copper pot still allows the rentention of the strong congeners — heads and tails — which impart flavor and rich aromas.

X.O. Brandy

In addition to the well known cognac letter designations as Three Star, V.S.O.P. and Napoleon, there is special designation for a full bodied, fruity spirit titled X.O. Hennessy, X.O. Cognac and the Christian Brothers X.O. Brandy as examples of this complex, rich distillate.

Calvados

Calvados is named from the Normandy town in northern France where it is made by distilling the cider of fine, ripe apples. In America, we call the product Apple-Jack. However, the Normans pot-distill their cider and age it up to ten years in wood, making incomparable apple brandy — CALVADOS!

Caramel in Spirits

Since all spirits emerge pure white in color, and many spirits gain differing hues in wood barrel aging, caramel is widely used to balance and maintain continuity in color in the bottled product. Really burnt sugar, caramel is tasteless and does not affect the spirit taste.
taste.

Cream Liqueur

For centuries, cordials and other cocktails were softened with fresh milk or cream. About four years ago, technological breakthroughs allowed the production and bottling of liquors directly with cream. The new category burst on the scene, to be dominated by the Irish. Real dairy cream, chocolate and other flavors make *creamy* delights.

When was Cognac First Aged?

When the Dutchman, William of Orange, assumed the throne of England, an alliance with Spain began which blocked wine and brandy trade from 1710 to 1714. Cognac makers were forced to store their spirits in barrels from local oak trees. When trade was resumed, the cognac was found to be *improved by the aging!*

Three Star Cognac

The three star designation in French brandy assures that the spirit is at least two years old — and nothing else. Those of greater age carry the letters VSOP or XO. Remember simply that the youngest of commercial cognacs all carry the 3 Star designation.

Five Star Cognac

Cognac is that brandy produced and aged in the Charente Province in Southeastern France. No other brandy throughout the world can be Cognac. The stars on the bottles denote relative quality in terms of wood aging before bottling. Three stars means 3 to 5 year old brandy. The best is the five stars meaning seven or more years of age!

Chartreuse

The only liqueur of commercial importance still under the jurisdiction of a religious order is the popular Chartreuse. Produced since 1607 in France and Spain, this sweet concoction is said to contain up to 140 herbs, plants and spices in a super-secret formula. Green Chartreuse is sold at 100 proof and lighter yellow at 86 proof. Try this brandy based cordial to finish a perfect evening.

Cointreau

Probably the world's best known and loved liqueur is named after its founders Adolphe and Edouard Cointreau. Made since 1849 in the Loire Valley, there are now 13 plants worldwide producing the light and sweet, 90 proof cordial from sweet and bitter orange peels.

Color in Liquors

All distilled liquors are light or white in color, the fewer the congeners the lighter the distillate. Aging in charred oak barrels lends a golden hue to bourbons. The addition of a small amount of caramel syrup at the time of rectification creates the pleasing hue in rum, brandy, whiskey and even some tequilas!

Congener

If you understand the role of the congener, you will easily appreciate the differences and likenesses in the range of liquors. Congeners are traces of oils, esters and acids passed over the fermentation and distillation of liquors. The lower the proof, the more the congeners. In sum, they are the taste and aroma characteristics that distinguish one type from another.

Cordial

In Latin *cordis* means heart. According to Heronymous Braunschweig, published in 1520, the earliest use of cordials or liqueurs was to stimulate the heart and lighten the spirit. The beverages were compounded of liquors and sweeteners to make palatable the often bitter medicines. Those doctors had heart!

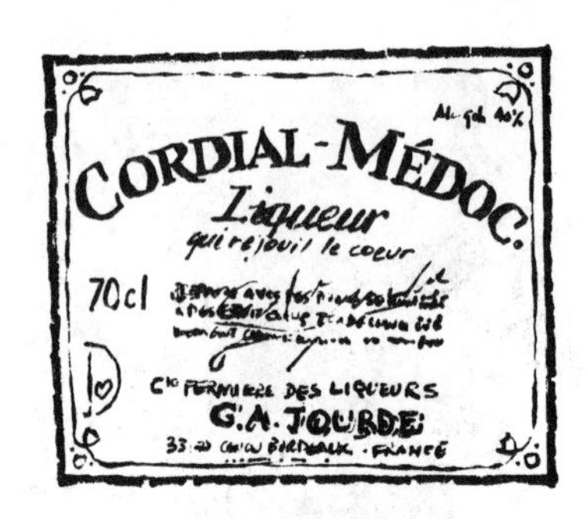

Cordial Medoc

Cordial Medoc literally means a liqueur from the Medoc area of the Bordeaux wine region. This concoction is a cocktail of liqueurs containing cognac, chocolate flavored creme de cacao and the popular orange flavored curacao, as well as a touch of claret. Sold at 88 proof, it is a powerful salute to the French!

Creme

Literally, creme means cream! Hence, logically, cremes are the very rich, fruity, creamy and oh-so-sweet cordials which are perfect as dessert toppings. Often low in alcohol, cremes are used in crushed ice as frappe' desserts.

Curacao

Oranges are a gift of the Orient that found delightful acceptance in Middle Ages in Europe. Curacao is a romantic island of the Indies noted for a particularly bitter orange. In making these fine liqueurs such as Curacao and Cointreau, only the peel is used for its aromatic oil. The liqueur is wonderfully bitter-sweet.

How was the Daiquiri Named?

Around the turn of this century, an enterprising American engineer named Jennings Cox was employed in the copper mines in Cuba. Cox would entertain visitors with the local toddy employing native rum, lime juice and sugar. Eventually Cox tabbed the tangy delight a Daiquiri after a nearby village.

Dead Man's Hand

Wild Bill Hickock loved to drink and gamble. On the fateful afternoon of August 3, 1876 he was doing both when shot in the head by Jack McCall in Deadwood, South Dakota. His last hand — black Aces and Eights — became the curse of the Dead Man's Hand.

Digestif

The French have a word for everything, including liqueurs. Digestifs for hundreds of years have been used after full meals as stomach restoratives. The fine bitters and cordials made of barks, quinine and seeds have done the job. *Vive le digestif!*

Distilling

The alchemist may have failed in his search of gold, but he perfected the art of distillation. Heat is applied to wine or beer and the ethyl alcohol vaporizes to be cooled as a hard liquor. Vive le Difference!

Triple Distilling

Once called the "whiskey of gentle authority" the spirits distilled on Erin Isle are indeed unique. But, it isn't the gift of Irish laughter but the triple distilling which renders the end product so light and airy. The three-fold distillation assures a lightness and purity excellent for sipping and superb with coffee!

Falernum

Now that rum is again returning to the American scene, you may find a recipe which calls for a touch of Falernum. Unrelated to the Ancient Roman wine called Falerno, it is quite simply a syrup from the West Indies. Invented several hundred years ago, it is made by adding six percent alcohol to molasses syrup, lime, almonds, ginger and other spices. The perfect rum companion.

Colonial Flip

Devotees of the modern flip appreciate their liquor smoothed with egg; sweetened with sugar; and topped with nutmeg. These are far from the original Colonial Flips which used strong beer, molasses, dried pumpkin and a shot of rum — all stired up with a hot poker!

Charcoal Filtering

Charcoal filters have the enviable capacity to remove undesirable elements from fluids. While used generously in whiskey-making, this technique is employed sparingly by winemakers particularly to remove color pigmentation when white wines have rested too long on their skins. Unfortunately, wine character is also lost!

Fish House Punch

This popular Colonial punch recipe was created in a famous social club of the same name formed in 1732 in Schuykill, Pennsylvania. Ideally blended hours or even days before consumption, the recipe calls for generous portions of rum, brandy, peach liqueur, loaf sugar, citrus juice, water and ice for cold service. No wonder its lasting popularity!

Fraise

Fraise or Creme de Fraise is a sweet, rich cordial with the flavor and aroma of fresh, ripe strawberries. Light red in hue, it is produced both from wild and cultivated fruit. The berries are macerated or soaked in alcohol to capture the delicate flavors and then distilled. Try Fraise with fruits and light cookies for dessert. You will love it.

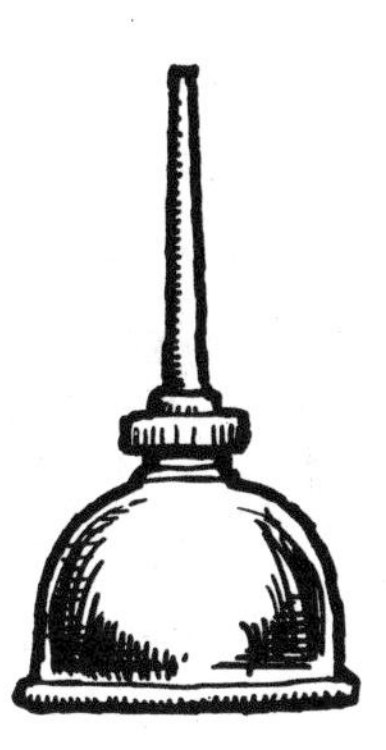

Fusel Oil

Fusel oils are congeners composed of higher alcohols present in most spirits — wines, liqueurs and liquors. In trace quantities, propyl, butyl, hexly and heptyl alcohols provide the sharp, volatile tastes. Fusel oils provide the distinctive bite in bourbon or cognac, the taste you remember.

Gill

Sailors in His Majesty's Navy in the seventeenth century were guaranteed two gills of rum each noon. A gill is the equivalent of five ounces, attesting to the formidable consumption aboard early sailing vessels.

Gin

Good old Dutch professor Sylvius distilled grain spirits over fresh juniper berries for medicinal purposes. In the 17th century, British soldiers shortened the word to gin and spread its effect throughout the empire. In addition to the tart juniper, other herbs used include cassia bark, fennel, almond, licorice and orange peel.

Gin Botanicals

The most universal of all spirits in terms of ingredients must be gin! Originally named for the predominant botanical — the juniper berry — gin often contains essences of as many as a dozen spices. Angelica from Europe; coriander from Czechoslovakia; orange peel from Spain; cardamon from Ceylon. These and many others are introduced in a second distillation making gin the universal drink!

Hollands Gin

The popular Long Dry Gin is produced by redistilling neutral grain spirits over Juniper berry essences. The Dutch produce Hollands gin, sometimes called Genever, by using malty grain spirits. It's a heavy aromatic sipping drink, like cognac!

London Dry Gin

Following nearly 150 years of consuming limitless quantities of heavily sugared and flavored gins, in 1850 there came into being in London a new perfectly sugarless gin. The dry refers to the lack of sugar. London dry gin has a crisp, juniper berry flavor popular in mixed drinks.

Plymouth Gin

The Royal British Navy not only ruled the seas for centuries, it carried abundant supplies of a dry but full bodied, pungent gin made in the seaside town of Plymouth. A Malty gin, with smoothness gained from the Devon waters, Plymouth was often mixed with Angostura bitters to make the famous "Pink Gin".

Old Tom Gin

Old Tom was an enterprising British agent who made a sideline living dispensing gin through a funnel in his front door — probably the first recorded automat. In his name, Old Tom Gin is known throughout the world as a slightly sweet, English Gin. There is nothing dry about Old Tom!

Sloe Gin

Neither slow, nor truly gin, this luscious brandy based, sweet, red cordial is made from sloe berries. The tiny purple plum berries grow on blackthorn bushes. The cordial has a flowery melon aroma and a tart almondy taste. Try a sloe gin fizz for trothy delight.

Grenadine

Since it is often found in cocktail recipes, many consider Grenadine an alcoholic liqueur. To the contrary, it is simply a smoothly sweet syrup concocted from pomegranates, strawberries, raspberries and similar fruits. It blends best with whiskey.

Grog

Grogram was a popular heavy cloth in the 1700's made from silk and wool. One popular British Admiral named Edward Vernon wore a distinctive grogram coat. Vernon began to dilute with water, the daily ration of rum he gave his sailors. They affectionately named the new drinks Old Grog!

Heads and Tails

Unlike the moonshiner, the modern whiskey distiller does not allow chance to determine his heads and tails. The heads and tails — foreshots and feints — are the most critical elements in his products — the tastes. These traces of esters, oils, acids and exotic higher alcohols are retained in controlled portions for flavor and bouquet.

Highball

In the last century station managers signaled the need for more speed to passing trains by holding aloft a stick with a ball on the end. Hence, speeding trains were highballing. Since the engineers favorite drink was bourbon and water, by 1890 the drink became known as a highball.

Hogshead

To mix a metaphor, the hogshead was the workhorse of the middle ages. In all its many forms and sizes, these barrels replaced the amphora as the common vessel for shipping fluids — wine, brandy, beer or oil. In Bordeaux it was called a Barrique, in Burgundy a Piece, in Spain a Butt.

Juniper Berry

One of the commonest of evergreen shrubs throughout the world is the juniper. There are thirteen species in the United States alone. The berry which grows on the female plant secretes an oil similar to the hop cone used in beer. The juniper berry oil is the dominant flavoring in gin along with many other herbs such as anise, licorice, coriander and caraway. In fact the word gin is a corruption of the Dutch word for juniper — Genever!

Kir

The mayor of the Burgundian town of Dijon during the Second World War was a priest by the name of Canon Kir. His favorite cocktail consisted of four parts of local white wine with one part of local black currant liqueur called Cassis. The low alcohol, aromatic Cassis enlivens the wine. You'll love a Kir!

Kirschwasser

Kirsch or kirschwasser is a high proof, colorless and completely dry brandy distilled from the small black cherry indigenous to central Europe. Do not mistake it for the popular very sweet Creme de Kirsch. The cherry is nearly as universal as the grape in its food and liquor uses!

Leaching

The singular distinction of fine Tennessee Whiskey is its mellow finish. This results from leaching the freshly distilled spirit though burned and ground hard Tennessee maple. It literally takes ten days for the whiskey to leach its way through twelve feet of pea sized charcoal.

Le Part Des Anges

The brandy called cognac is aged for years in warehouses called Chais above ground unlike wine caves. About three percent of the precious fluid evaporates from the barrels filling the air in Cognac town with the equivalent of 12 million bottles of brandy per year. The French say it is The Angels Share!

Limestone Water

As Scotch and Irish immigrant farmers moved westward to to the hills of Kentucky, they discovered more than fertile soil. The fresh cold waters flowing from rocky springs were nearly mineral free. The limestone shelf extending to Tennessee, Illinois and through Kentucky purifies the water — and iron free water makes good whiskey! Little wonder Bourbon caught on!

Liqueur

Originally medicinal remedies and nostrums, cordials or liqueurs are mixtures of liquor — usually brandy — with pleasant flavors including fruits, peels, pits, seeds, leaves and spices. Always sweet, sometimes very sweet, nice for desserts.

Liquer d'Or

A delight among the profusion of French herbal liqueurs is d'or. The word refers to the quite visible flecks of pure gold suspended in the fluid. Made from lemon peels, herbs and plants, d'or is reminiscent of yellow Chartreuse with a mysterious, lingering finish on the palate.

Liquor Tax

Man's pleasures and follies are prime targets of the tax collector. The first excise tax on whiskey was imposed in 1791 to help defray the enormous debts of the Revolution. The first tax of less than a cent a gallon rose to $6.40 during World War I and to the present $10.50. It is a major source of federal dollars.

Maceration

Liqueur maceration is the age old technique of infusing rich fruit aromas and tastes into after-dinner cordials. High proof spirits, usually brandies, are placed in a tank with the crushed fruit pulp. The mixture is steeped, like tea, for days or months creating a glorious wedding of interests!

Mandarine

Most of the familiar citrus fruit liqueurs are made from sweet and bitter orange peels. A popular exception is Mandarine developed from sweet tangerines. Bright orange in color, overwhelmingly sweet, it is best used as a cocktail or punch flavoring.

Maraschino

Tart maraschino cherries from Dalmatia, Yugoslavia are used to make this bitter-sweet delight. The cherry stones are distilled separately to be combined with pomace of the fruit. Aged in neutral hickory wood, Maraschino is sold often in wicker bottles.

Marc

The oldest and most universal of all spirit brandies is eau-de-vie-de-marc. Marc is the pomace or pulp left after wine has been fermented and racked. In the Burgundy area, it traditionally was packed under clay until mid-winter; watered; and refermented before distilling. Many well known vineyards produce this marc including Romanee-Conti, Musigny and Chambertin.

Margarita

The Margarita, the trademark of Tequila drinking, was invented by a Mexican bartender who had a girlfriend very fond of salt. He solved her problem by twisting the glass in salt first, adding tequila and Cointreau and the juice of a local fruit called the limon.

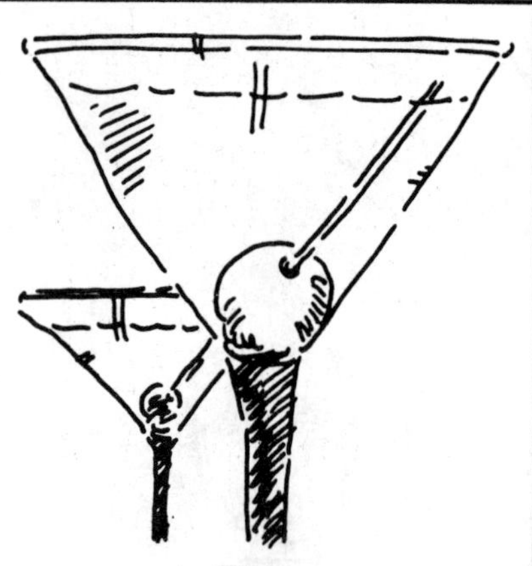

Dry Martini

It may be surprising but the first martini — named for a gentleman named Martinez — was fifty-fifty gin and sweet vermouth. At the turn of this century, the Knickerbocker Hotel in New York offered a version using Dry Gin and as little as one eighth dry vermouth in the glass. The Dry Martini was born.

Mash

There is no record of when man first discovered the magical effects of steeping grain in hot water. Chemically, the enzyme diastase converts the grain starches to fermentable sugars. The fermented mash becomes beer and the distilled beer becomes whiskey. It all begins with the mash.

Mead

Mead was the favorite drink of the Anglo-Saxon. This soft concoction may even have preceded grape wine and is in a class by itself being neither fruit nor grain in origin. Honey and water are allowed to ferment, often with flavoring herbs to produce luscious mead.

Mescal Azul

Among the several hundred species of the agave plant, the Mescal Blue or Tequilana Weber is the prized plant used in the production of Tequila. Its blue, swordlike leaves protect a Pina heart of sugar from which the alcohol is produced. Grown only in the Jalisco Province of Mexico, and Azul is the source of all Tequila.

Mezcal

If Tequila is the gentle spirit of the Mexican nobleman, Mezcal is the drink of the peon. Like Tequila, it is produced from a variety of cactus called the Dumpling. Following a short fermentation of the juice and heart, there is single distillation. The spirit sold at 100 proof is aid to contain traces of the hallucinogen mescaline!

Moonshine

Moonshine is the raw, unaged liquor often called "mountain dew" which is produced on illegal stills often of very low quality. As early as the 18th century, illegal brandy or gin smuggled into England and Ireland was termed moonshine. Five thousand illegal stills were seized in 1973 alone and billions in taxes have been lost due to these clandestine enterprises. To be certain, buy legitimate!

Mull

Before central heating, warding off winter's chill took on many forms. The mull was a favorite warmer. Basically, mulls are sugared and spiced hot drinks made from a base of wine, beer or cider. For effect, brandy, rum and aquavit were added either singly or together. Little wonder our forefathers had a tendency to "mull over" thorny questions!

Muy Anejo

Most everyone recognizes popular Tequila as a light, colorless nearly neutral spirit that mixes easily in any drink. Small amounts of Tequila are aged in used whiskey barrels acquiring a soft, golden hue. Two or more years in wood is Muy Anejo!

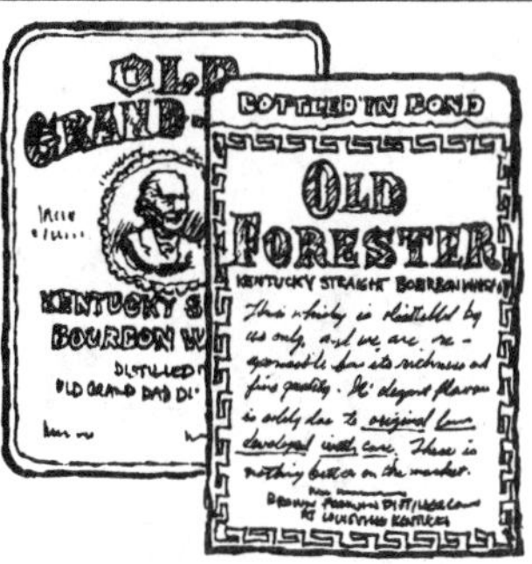

How Old Are National Brands?

A combination of factors brought brand identification to the American spirits field. Until the turn of this century, most spirits were dispensed from barrels. Often they were diluted or adulterated. The advent of the automatic bottler in 1903 and the desire to maintain quality combined with the 1909 Pure Food and Drug Act to create now familiar brand names.

Neutral Spirit

Do not be misled that neutral spirits are any less potent than those familiar liquors containing the smells and tastes of the grains or fruits. A neutral spirit by law is ethyl alcohol taken from the still at 190 proof or above — that is 95 percent pure ethanol without a discernable trace of the grain or other distilling material. Vodka is normally a neutral spirit diluted with distilled water.

Oak Char

The inside of a bourbon whiskey barrel of new oak has been blackened over raging gas fires. The resulting layers of dark char, soft carmel and pure oak combine as catalysts for chemical aging and produce both tart flavor and ruddy hue. They allow air in for oxidizing and water out.

Limousin Oak

An extraordinary marriage of nature is the Quercus Robur — hard oaks — of the Limousin forests and the distillation called Cognac from nearby provinces. In the late middle ages, this oak was chosen to hold the young brandy. Soon was observed an unusual mellowing effect on long stored spirits. Some cognac is now aged up to twenty years! Limousin oaks imparts special character to spirits or wines unmatched by other woods throughout the world.

Ocha

An unusual and pleasing liqueur comes to us from Japan. Also sometimes called Suntory Green Tea Liqueur, Ocha is produced by steeping bitter, rolled tea leaves in brandy and neutral spiritis. Retaining the tea bitterness, Ocha contains up to fifty percent sugar for a very sweet finish.

Oke

Sojourners to our Fiftieth state soon become acquainted with Okolehao, a favorite local spirit taken on the rocks or in highball form. Distilled from a mash compounded of the sacred Ti plant, molasses and rice, Oke is sold in Crystal Clear and Golden hues at 80 proof. It is the liquid Lei!

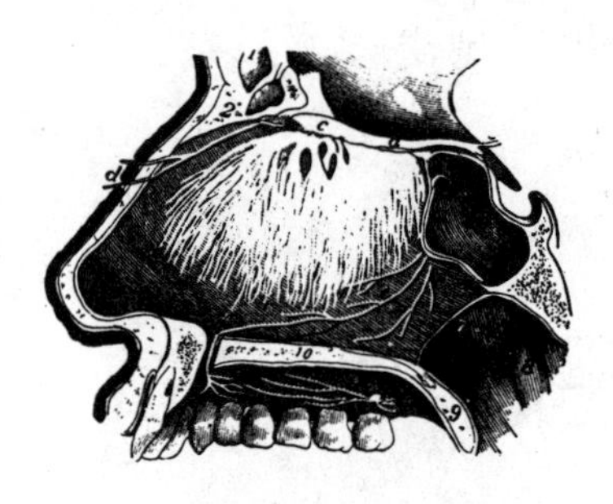

What is the Olfactory Sense

While man is limited to four tastes, he can distinguish up to ten thousand odors. Molecules are volatized as vapors and they are carried up the nasal passages to the olfactory nerves. The brain reacts favorably or is repulsed. Hence the sense of smell is integral to the enjoyment of beverage alcohols.

Orgeat

Ever wonder what magic that bartender is working back there? A universal sweetener at the back bar is known as orgeat. A syrup, orgeat was originally made from barley but is now often fabricated from sugar, almonds and milk with a touch of brandy. It adds life to any drink!

Ouzo

Ouzo is the pungent, anise flavored liqueur of the Greek. Reminiscent of French Pernod, it is sold at ninety proof and is brandy based. It is best served with very cold water — about four ounces of water to one of Ouzo. It blends milky white and is a refreshing aperitif or dessert.

Pastis

Pastis is the happy successor to universally banned Absinthe. Concocted from neutral spirits and herb flavorings, the dominant flavor is from aniseed. A favorite of French fishermen, it is usually diluted with water or served over the ice. A superb thirstquencher!

Peat Reek

When something is overpowering in odor, it is common to say it "reeks". This is literally true for Scotch whiskey revered world-wide for its smoky flavor. The ground barley malt is dried over heaps of burning peat acquiring the acrid oily flavor unique to Scotch.

Percolation

The liqueur maker utilizes the exact process as the coffee maker to extract the oils and essences for his luscious cordials. The seeds,leaves or beans are placed in a basket. A combination of water and alcohol is repeatedly pumped over the flavor agents extracting the delightful tastes.

Persico

Persico is an oh-so-light cordial which dates back to 18th Century England made from fresh peaches. The delicate peach flavor is lighter and more difficult to capture in liquors than many other fruits. Therefore the peach is more often used as an accent to other juices in cordials as in the popular Southern Comfort.

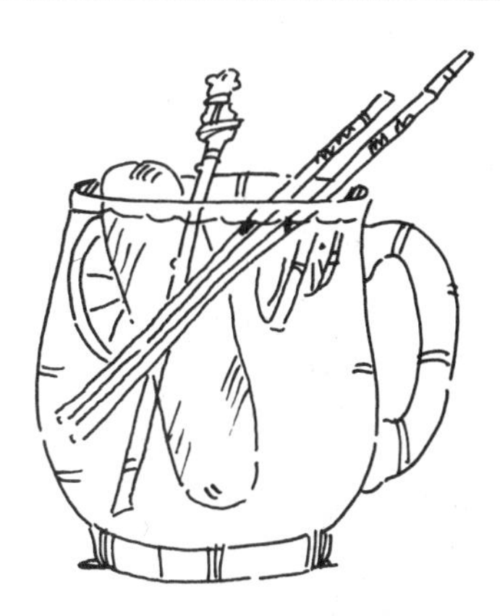

Pimms Cup

Perhaps the most famous of all mixed drinks was originated nearly two hundred years ago in a London restaurant. In preparing his gin slings, the proprietor added a touch of herbs and a dash of Continental liqueur. They became so popular that the secret formulation was bottled and is popular yet today.

Pina

The heart of the Blue Agave plant grown extensively in Mexico and South America is termed a pina — or pineapple which it closely resembles. It takes up to ten years to mature the plant pina which under steaming and pressure will yield up to 30 pounds of molasses. Fermented and distilled this pina juice is called tequila.

Pineau Des Charentes

A worker's accident some four hundred years ago led to the most popular aperitif-liqueur in Southern France. Pineau des Charentes is produced only in the Cognac region and is made by blending new cognac brandy into fresh grape juice. Then aged like fine brandy, Pineau is clean and fruity as an aperitif over ice! It is the only aperitif under the Appelation Controlee.

Pisco

Pisco is grape brandy, distilled from mellow muscat grapes near the port town of Pisco in Southern Peru. Appreciated world-wide, its fame grew from celebrated Pisco Punch in gold rush days of San Francisco. It is unaged, pure white and fiery. Try it in a sour!

Planters Punch

Planters Punch truly wedded the Far East with the New West of the sixteenth century. The new aromatic rum of the Caribbean was blended with the citrus from the Orient. To make a Planters Punch, remember the old ditty, "One of sour (lime), two of sweet (sugar), three of strong (rum) and four of weak (ice cubes).

Poire William

The most distinctive of all fruit brandy is that distilled from ripe Williams and Bartlett pears. Though very difficult to ferment and distill, the resulting spirit has intense fruit aroma and delicate taste. A beautiful aperitif!

Potato Spirit

It is no myth that white spirits are produced from fresh potatoes. Since the 18th century, the Swedes and Danes have produced Aquavit and Akvavit from the nutritious tubers since they are so much cheaper than grain in Scandinavia. Most of this vodka-like drink is flavored with caraway and other herbs.

Poteen

To an Irishman, a poteen is a small pot. It is also illegal whiskey produced in small pot stills over untold centuries in hidden bogs of that romantic land. Descendants of these poteen makers settled in the hills of Kentucky and created American moonshine!

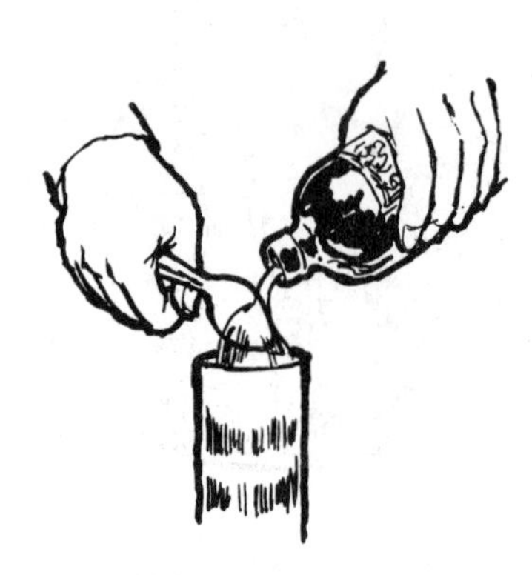

Pousse-Cafe

Showy Pousse-Cafe drinks are formed by floating layers of Liqueurs. Pour over an inverted teaspoon and they may be prepared and refrigerated in advance. Try a Patriotic — first red Creme de Noyaux; next white Creme de Menthe and then glistening blue Curacao. Salute!

Pouilly Fuisse'

The almost unpronounceable, newly popular white wine from France is named for two close hamlets — Pouilly and Fuisse'. Very dry like the Chablis to the north, it is produced from the elegant Chardonnay grape and is excellent with any light entree.

Proof

American proof is twice the actual alcohol content. 100 proof bourbon has 50% alcohol. 200 proof is pure alcohol. Wine, which shows 12% alcohol By Volume on the label is, therefore, 24 proof.

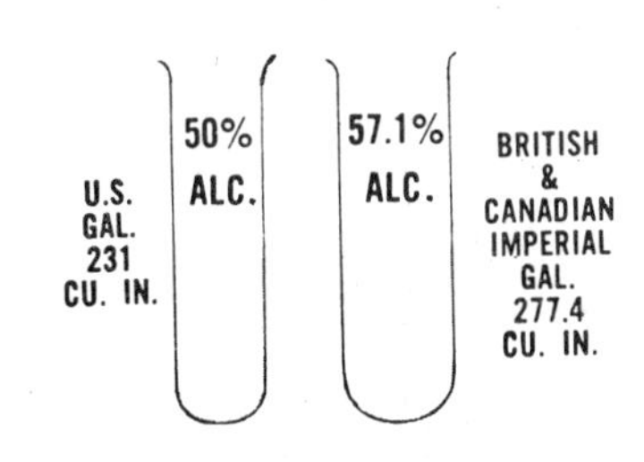

Proof Gallon

The inventor of the hydrometer left a legacy of confusion for the alcohol consumer. He named the alcohol as proof where the hydrometer floated — at the odd level of 57.1% of alcohol by volume. Fortunately or not, our federal officials changed the formula of proof to exactly half of the volume as alcohol — hence a proof gallon. Confused? So is everyone else but the tax collector!

Gunpowder Proof

The confusing term proof originated innocently enough from the practice of early booze peddlers giving proof of alcohol in their blends. Equal parts of gunpowder and the liquor were lit with a match. At exactly fifty percent alcohol, a nice blue flame resulted. Hence proof today is twice the actual alcohol content.

Highest Proof Liquor

If you are looking for high proof, look to imported rums. Some is sold up to 151 proof, and that is seventy five and one half percent pure ethanol. The remaining fluid is mostly water thought it has chemical traces of the molasses it was made from.

Proprietary Cordial

In the late sixteenth century, the cordial became a significant beverage. At this period most were mixtures of brandy and exotic herbs, flowers and spices desired for their delicate shades in taste. The secret recipes could not be easily copied so names such as Chartreuse or Benedictine survived as unique products — purchased only from the proprietary firm. Proprietary labels command a large and growing share of the market.

Ratafia

Ratafia originally were the sweet drink concoctions made to drink at the signing of treaties. A whole series of aperitifs came to be called Ratafia usually made with soft fruit like raspberries or strawberries. A few are still produced in France like Ratafia de Bourgogne and Ratafia de Champagne.

Retsina

Since ancient times, the Greeks have flavored wines with pine resin. Nearly half of the white and rose' wines produced for local consumption are thusly treated. Try one as an aperitif or a conversation piece. But, recognize Retsina as an acquired taste!

Rock and Rye

Old wives tales were based on practical observations. One of the most satisfying was a dose of Rock and Rye as a nostrum for the common cold. The rye was rye whiskey, the rock was a combination of lemons, oranges, cherries and other fresh fruits and rock candy syrup. Old wives noticed the pleasant results from this liqueur.

Rum

The blood thirsty pirate, the proper British soldier, and the American colonist shared a partiality for Rum. Rum is made from cane sugar. Picked; crushed; boiled to molasses; fermented; and finally distilled into rum. Light rum is enjoying a new popularity in our nation.

Barbados Rum

As early as 1775, our forefathers consumed prodigious amounts of West Indies Rum. The Barbados Island soil is composed of volcanic ash and yields a cane sugar molasses which transforms into a heavy, smokey rum. It is best sipped and savored as compared to the light Puerto Rican types!

Martinique Rum

Because of its unique characteristics, rum made Martinique the richest of all the Caribbean Isles. Very much like American and Jamaican rums, Martinique is bold, flavorful and possessed of delightful bouquet. Try it over the rocks or as a flambe'!

Puerto Rican Rum

The national trend to light and white in beverage alcohol has lifted rum to widespread popularity. The lightest and the whitest of rums are made from molasses all over the Island of Puerto Rico. The Silver or White label type is the lightest of all and it outsells its fellow Golden Rum three bottles to one. Puerto Rican — the mixable, fixable rum!

Rum Types

Of all beverage spirits, rums retain the greatest identity with their source material — molasses! Light Puerto Rican rum is fermented in half a day and distilled to high proof. Deep, dark Jamaican rums are fermented up to a week and distilled to heavy pungency in pot stills. So, pick your rum carefully and expect diversity in aroma and taste. You won't be disappointed!

Schnapps

The most popular distilled spirit in the Scandinavian countries and in Germany is called Schnapps. It is the continental vodka.Made from potatoes or grain, it is white and neutral to the taste. In Hanover, they drink their beer and schnapps at the same time, artfully spilling one into the other on the way!

Peppermint Schnapps

What a delight and what a difference is Peppermint Schnapps. To anyone who has quaffed the dry, fiery Germanic Schnapps, the cordial glass of the peppermint flavored variety is a new and rewarding experience. Try this one with mints and nuts after a full meal.

Scotch

The Scots claim to have first distilled a malted grain in 1505 called Usquebaugh — later shortened to whisky. The key to the smoky scotch taste is literally the smoke of peat bog logs which are used to dry the malt. Scotch is a blend of many whiskies and is generally aged up to ten years. A truly unique spirit.

Scotch Blend

The true afficionado of scotch whisky should appreciate the long term and infinitely subtle steps that create distinctive scotch blends. As many as forty different aging whiskys about four years old are tested in standard wine glasses by sight, smell and taste. The light Highland and Lowland spirits predominate with accent from the pungent Campbelltown and Islay malts. Further aging follows the artful blending.

Single Malt Scotch

Once the pride of all Scotsmen, a single malt scotch is now a rarity around the world. Popular scotches are blends of up to fifty whiskys and spirits. The base of these blends is always the fiery and hundred percent barley malt whisky — the single malt. A great sipper like cognac!

Singapore Sling

The earliest known record of a Sling was in 1768 in Colonial America. Gin was then at the height of its popularity in the British Empire. The gin was mixed with sweetened water, not unlike the highball of today. The Singapore Sling survives today little changed as the first, formal cocktail.

Slivovitz

A favorite delicate liquor in Yugoslavia and other Eastern European nations is the plum brandy called Slivovitz. It is unique among fruit brandies as it is aged in wood barrels up to twelve years. This aging creates a straw color and slightly woody taste.

Southern Comfort

Bourbon is the base for this popular, luscious, peach flavored liqueur which has satisfied thousands since the civil war. Made popular again in Gone With The Wind, it provides a clean finish on the palate with moderate sweetness. Perfect for a mixer!

First American Spirit

The world's oldest distilled spirit — Rum — was also the first commercial American spirit. About 1650, molasses from the Barbados was distilled to New England rum. John Adams wrote, "Molasses was an essential ingredient in American independence."

Steinhager

In Westphalia, Germany, the favorite drink is laced with the local gin called Steinhager. Sold in stoneware crocks that emphasize its strong juniper overtone, it most resembles a strong London Dry Gin.

Continuous Still

Invented by a thrifty Scot liquor trader in 1832, the continuous still is basically a series of pot stills one upon the other. It has the very considerable financial advantage of running all day long with new product and of taking the liquor at any proof desired. Steam strips the alcohol from the beer or wine as it passes through.

Pot Still

Distilling in its most fundamental form is accomplished — as any moonshiner knows — by applying wood fire or steam heat to wine or beer held in a pot. A funnel-like head directs the rising ethyl alcohol fumes through a cooling condenser and then to a jug. The resulting fluid is a hard liquor or the distilled spirit of the wine or beer in the tank.

Simple Syrup

Simple syrup is simply done, but it is the reason for the creamy consistency of bar made specialty drinks and professional liqueurs. Simply boil a cup of water for a few seconds to boil out impurities and then add a cup of sugar. Simmer two minutes and you have a simple syrup!

Tail Box

The Kentucky moonshiner and the French Cognac distiller share a common production advantage. Both use the pot still which allows periodic tasting of the brandy or bourbon as it drips from the condenser. The modern distiller must depend upon a hydrometer enclosed in a "tail box" beyond touch or taste and under federal control. What price progress!

Teetotaler

In the latter half of the nineteenth century, the fuss and fury over prohibition rose to an emotional crescendo. The Laingsburg, Michigan Temperance Society offered two options in the form of Pledges. The first promised moderate drinking. The preferred second pledge of total abstinance was recorded with a "T." These enlistees for TEETOTALERS!

Tequila

A light bodied liquor from cultivated agave cactus plants from central Mexico. The artichoke-like heart is mashed and fermented before distilling. A great cocktailer — as in Margarita!

Triple Sec

Perhaps the most common of all cordials is Triple Sec. It is produced in many countries using the bittersweet oils in orange peels. Twist a peel over a flame and these oils will spark and burn. For sipping or as a cocktail ingredient, Triple Sec is smooth and satisfying!

Tuaca

For a mellow, orange and coconut creamy liqueur, try the very old Tuaca label from Italy. With the crest of the Medici family on the label, this milk and brandy based cordial was a favorite of Lorenzo the Magnificent in the year 1492. That's durability, and it will provide a gracious finish to a fine meal today as well!

Uisge Beatha

The first whiskey of man is thought to have originated in the rolling hills of Ireland. Irish legend even claims St. Patrick as the first whiskey maker. As early as the tenth century, mention is found in Gaelic of Uisge Beatha, or water of life. The Irish have a word for it!

Vatting

Veteran Scotch drinkers recognize the difference between blends and single malt Scotch whiskey. The latter is mellowed and blended with neutral spirits. The single malt is the pure Highland barley spirits, a delight in itself. Distillers simply mix two or more single malts in the VATTING PROCESS. Sometimes they sell this as ALL MALT WHISKEY!

Vodka

The Russian's "dear little water" has become the favorite potable spirit of the American citizen. Vodka is truly the least of all potables as it is taken from the still above 190 retaining nothing of the taste and smell of the grain. This neutrality and ability to mix with anything has propelled Vodka to the top of the charts!

V.S.O.P.

The V.S.O.P. designation is found on cognac labels and other French Brandies. In Cognac, there is a bewildering array of items to classify the brandy. Very Superior Old Pale — V.S.O.P. — is a step better than Three Star Cognac.

Whiskey Aging

Whiskey aging is essentially a mellowing process; it is accomplished in wooden barrels which impart both color and tannin to the spirits. Charred oak barrels are essential to bourbon while softer used barrels create the light Canadian blends. Once bottled, aging ceases!

Whiskey Bead

Never at a loss for a measure of value, the early whiskey consumer learned to take a bead on the quality of his purchase. When poured in a glass or shaken in a jar, liquor should leave a string-like necklace of bubbles — the bead. The higher the proof, the longer lasting and more uniform the bead!

Blended Whiskey

Blended whiskey — like coffee, tea and tobacco — is a highly refined mix tailored to taste. Blends are works of art which provide the unique tastes to favorite brands. They may include light and heavy whiskies as well as neutral spirits and sherry. Praise to the blender!

Body in Whiskey

The body or thickness of any fluid is easily sensed on the tongue. In whiskey, the size of the original grain is the principle factor. The larger the grain, the lighter the resulting whiskey. Hence, Rye with small grain makes bigger bodied whiskey than the larger corn used in bourbon!

Bonded Whiskey

Don't be fooled by that stamp. Bottling in bond has nothing to do with quality. An Act in 1894 allowed distillers to skip immediate payment of taxes on bonded bottles. Your only guarantee is that it is straight whiskey, taken from the still below 160 proof, aged at least four years, and bottled at 100 proof. Despite all this, it's usually a bargain!

Canadian Whisky

Corn, rye, wheat and barley are used to make the Canadian distillates. However, as in Scotland, the Canadians drop the E from the end of the word and utilize used barrels which impart much softer flavors in aging. Canadian whisky is light and mellow.

Corn Whiskey

The distinctive taste of bourbon emanates from the mash and the new charred oak barrel aging. A country cousin of bourbon corn whiskey is of inestimably greater charm. Its ingredients must be eighty percent corn and the aging is accomplished in softer used barrels.

Grain Whiskey

Scotch, as it is sold throughout the world today, is dependent upon the heavy proportion of light grain whiskies. As opposed to the pungent, single malt whiskies, the grain types are taken from stills at a very high proof. As many as 30 malt whiskies and 5 grain whiskies are in every blend of Scotch.

Light Whiskey

Light whiskey is the American distillers answer to the lighter Canadian blends. Taken at the very high proof from 161 to 189 from the still and aged in used barrels like the Canadians, the whiskey obtains fewer wood extractives and a mixable taste. It's in the trend to lightness.

Rye Whiskey

Rye was the main crop of our industrious Scottish ancestors. They always set aside a portion for home distilling. Rye and barley produce the strongest tastes in whiskey. Rye whiskey must be produced at least 51 percent from rye grains. Expect the most in taste from Rye. You won't be disappointed!

Whiskey

The simplest definition of straight whiskey is that spirit taken directly from the still — as the white lightning of the moonshiner. Federal rules define straight whiskey as that distilled at 160 proof or under — assuring a strong character — which is aged two years in new charred oak barrels. The trend is away from this strong spirit to the blends and even lighter white spirits.

Sour Mash Whiskey

In sour mashing, each new batch of mash contains about 25% of spent mash from a completed distillation. The mash becomes innoculated then with a lactic culture and this, plus longer fermentation, produces the characteristic bitter-sweet taste in the whiskey.

Tennessee Whiskey

Though made with corn and distilled at low proof, Tennessee whiskey is distinct from bourbon. Its unique body and taste derive from a ten-day torturous journey down through a huge vat packed tight with maple tree charcoal. Try it over ice or sip straight.

Zubrovka

Zubrovka is the enormously popular Polish vodka. More like a liqueur than the pure white American vodkas. Zubrovka has an attractive yellow-green tint, a really earthy aroma and slightly bitter taste. All of these derive from soaking the spirit in native Zubra grass, and leaving a blade in the bottle!

PART THREE: Purchasing And Tasting Section

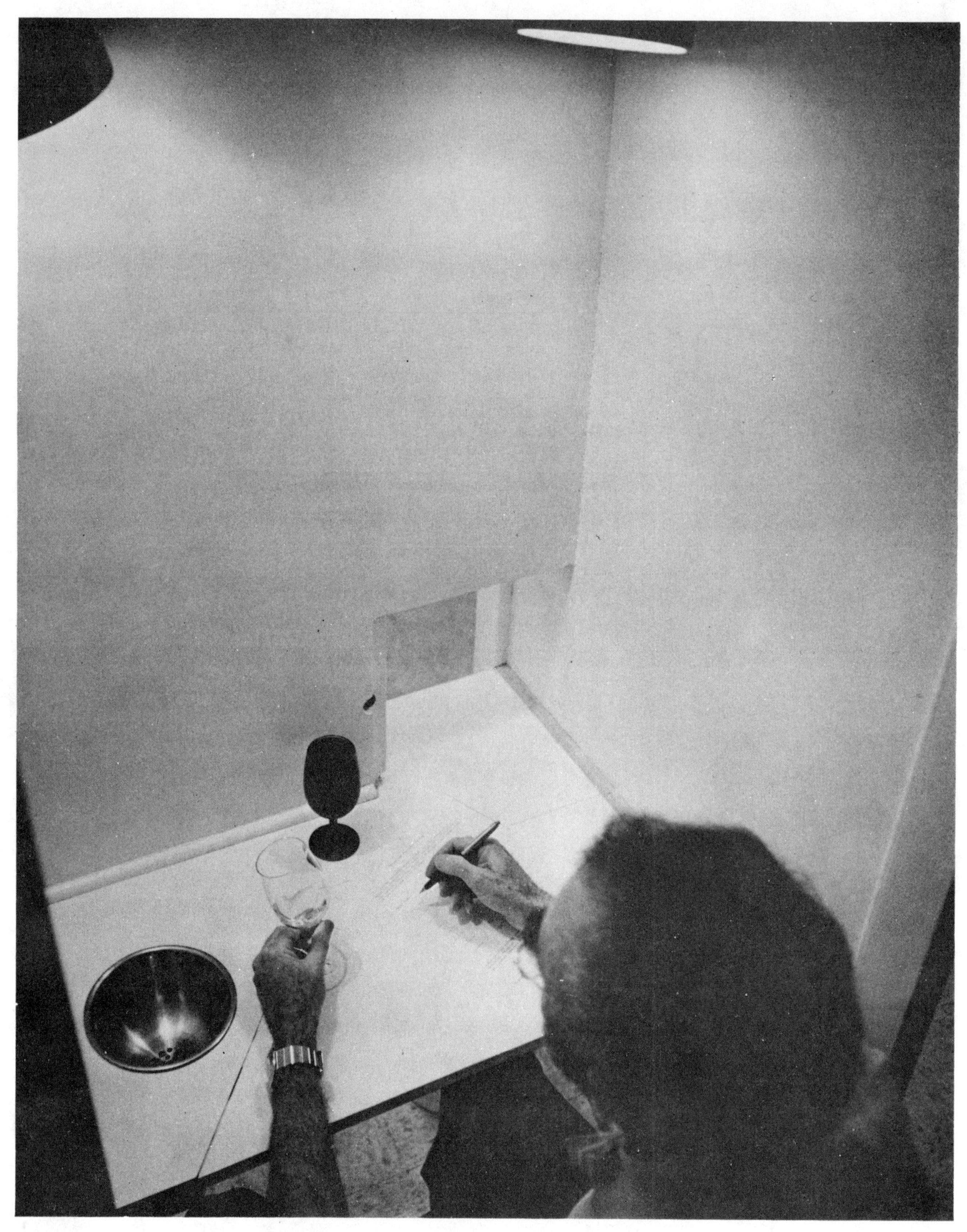

PROFESSIONAL TASTERS ALLOW NO DISTRACTIONS FROM THE WORK IN HAND (University of California, Davis)

Beverage Tasting Simplified

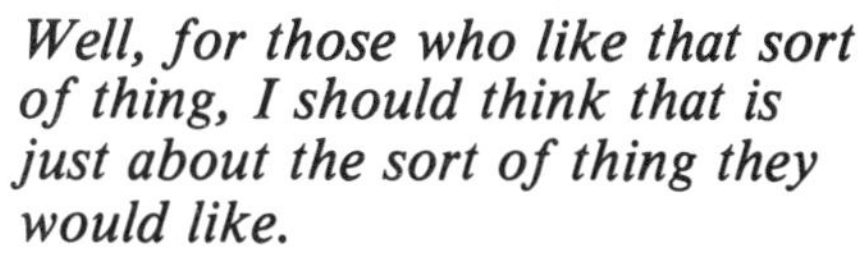

Well, for those who like that sort of thing, I should think that is just about the sort of thing they would like.

Abraham Lincoln

Everyone to his taste, as the woman said when she kissed her cow.

Rabelais

We are born with about ten thousand minute papillae or taste buds on the tongue, the roof of the mouth and in the throat. These sensors discern among tastes much as tiny fingers. As we age, the buds gradually diminish in sensitivity and even in number. The older we become, the less sensitive we are to the nuances of taste.

The tip and sides of the tongue respond to sweetness. Saltiness is perceived also near the front and on the sides of the tongue. The back and sides of the tongue and the roof of the mouth deliver both sourness and bitterness. Therein lies the whole complex world of taste — sweetness, sourness, bitterness and saltiness.

As we readily recognize, most foods provide a combination of two or more of these basic sensations. Apples are at once sweet and sour when ripe. Lemons are predominantly acidic or sour but there is an overtone of astringency or bitterness. The persimmon and strong tea are both strongly bitter, but are often consumed with a dash of sugar.

The mouth also warns us of heat and cold; rough and smooth; heavy and light. Syrup is full in body as water is light.

The hormone cortisone regulates taste. Since it flows more abundantly in the mornings, our tastes are more sensitive then. In addition, the buds fatigue easily and are almost as unpredictable as mood swings that afflict us through the day.

In wine and spirit tasting, we are concerned primarily with a *trio of tastes* — sweet, sour, and bitter — since saltiness is rare as a natural commodity in liquors.

AROMA AND BOUQUET

The olfactory or smell organs are located at the head of the nasal cavity. These extremely sensitive conductors react to molecular gases given off by thousands of objects about us, food included.

Yet, the line often blurs between taste and smell. Close your nostrils and you will have difficulty telling an apple from an onion. Flavor is considered to be a fusion of the two complimentary senses.

In wine and spirit tasting, we ascribe particular meaning to two nouns: aroma and bouquet. *Aroma* is the remaining odor of the original fruit or grain. Hence, the aroma of wine is grape smell. *Bouquet* is comprised of a host of odors which are created in the fermentation, distillation and aging processes.

While this may sound a bit technical, it is really quite natural. What we have done is to distinguish fresh fruit odors as aroma, and newly created odors as bouquet.

A TOTAL HUMAN RESPONSE

Professionals use the world "organoleptic" to describe the harmonious human response in tasting. Attention to all stimuli can heighten and expand upon the basic tastes and smells. Try to involve these three areas in your personal response to a wine or liquor.

Visual: the basic appearance, the sheen, clarity, the brillance, the trueness of color.

The Nose: the "grapey," or varietal character, in wine or fruit liquors, the smokiness in Scotch, the profusion in wine bouquet, from lilacs and strawberries to apples and pears, the intensity and persistence of each.

The Gustatory Response in the Mouth: the body or viscosity, the delicacy or sharpness, the harmony of flavors; the finish or aftertaste.

SOME COMMONLY USED TERMS IN TASTING

Appearance: overall clarity and sheen

Acidity: the presence of fruit acids as in oranges or grapefruit, the absence of acidity is flatness, and over-acidity is tartness.

Astringency or Bitterness: Astringency is a puckery feeling on the sides and the central portion of the tongue. This sensation is often confused with bitterness which is one of the four tastes. Both occur from the presence of tannin in wines. Distinguish astringency as a tactile feeling and bitterness as a taste.

Body: the thickness of the fluid, the heaviness on the tongue.

Balance: everything seems just right.

Dryness: the absence of sugar.

Flavor: distinct harmony in smell and taste.

Fruitiness: retention of the liveliness of the fruit flavors.

Medium dry to medium sweet: the growing concentration of sugar.

Quality: truly a subjective judgment.

Ford's Five Easy Steps For a Wine Or Brew Tasting Party

Wine is constant proof that God loves us, and loves to see us happy.

Benjamin Franklin

STEP ONE: Decide the Size

Every other decision depends upon the number of guests. Invite a few neighbors or an entire social club. You can plan about a half bottle per person over a two hour wine tasting. This presumes six or seven wines and slightly over an ounce per person for each selection. It will average out that way! And your major expense can be figured by planning one bottle of each type for each twenty guests.

STEP TWO: Pick the Place

Choose a patio, a room or a hall, if need be, that accommodates the expected guests and no more! There needs to be room for a supplies table in the entryway, an hors d'oeuvres table and, ideally, a table for each wine or beer being tasted. Allow for ease of movement, but create the crowd atmosphere. It will enliven your tasting!

STEP THREE: Pick The Wines *or brews*

This is an easier task than you might suspect. Since few people consume wine *or exotic brews* regularly in their homes, the average audience will be pleased whatever your choice. Here are a few suggestions:

Choose no more than seven or eight wines or brews.

Try a mix: three white, two rose, one sparking or in brews, try a range from light American lagers, to British ales, to Dutch and German lagers or specialty brews, and try one of the new American micro-brewery selections for differences.

For a wider selection of domestic and import brews, go to any large wine and spirit retail store, or ask the beverage manager in your favorite supermarket for a really broad range of brews. It is a good idea to buy a pocket guide to beer also since most of your guests will be unfamiliar with the many terms used on the labels which you select.

You can see the combinations are numerous. Whatever the choice, try to follow the rules for order of tasting: dry to sweet, white to red and light to heavy.

STEP FOUR: Assemble the Props

Tastings may be elaborate and formal, or simple and relaxed. Remember that the wine or beer is the featured attraction . . . and an enhancement for socializing with friends. Here are the basic materials you'll need:

- One wine glass per person. Glassware is ideal though plastic will do. Tasters keep their glasses through the tasting.

- Water pitchers and plastic spit buckets for each table so guests may rinse glasses if desired.

- Paper napkins in profusion.

- Pencils and pads, if you plan to rate the wines, or play tasting games.

- Xeroxed list of the wines in the suggested order of tasting with brief comments of what to look for in each. Consult the labels or book for descriptions.

- Morsels to clear the palate. These can range from simple breads and cheeses to elaborate canapes — whatever the budget allows — but avoid the spicy and salty.

- Decorate to suit your mood: posters, grapes, leaves.

STEP FIVE: Relax and Let the Wine Work Its Wonders

Don't make a big to-do, Tastings ought to be simple, casual, fun events. Allow your guests to socialize and to wander freely between the tables. Educate your servers on the basics of the wines and beers being tasted so they can make appropriate comments. Ask them to serve one ounce each time. Stand back and have a good time.

AN ELEGANT LAWN PARTY IN FAR OFF WASHINGTON STATE . . .
(Chateau Ste. Michelle)

Cheese and Wine . . . The Happy Marriage

Wine and cheese go together. They are kindred foods. Each can be a living, changing thing. Diversity is a hallmark of each. Each acquires treasured subtleties after fermentation has overcome humble beginnings. And each has fiery partisans for each of many varieties.

Bon Appe'tit

Bear in mind the same logical relationship between food and wine, and you triumph at the cheese board. A robust beef roast demands a full-bodied, tannic red wine for perfect companionship. A crab souffle works best with a spicy, slightly acidic white wine. The same rules apply with cheese.

The natural alkilinity in cheese is tempered by the abundant fruit acids in wine. In a manner of speaking all wines harmonize with all cheeses. However, you will discover a greater kinship if you marry the harder cheeses with the stronger wines. In like manner, the soft and creamy types fare best with lighter vintages. Finally, avoid sweets and other desserts which dull the taste buds.

Here are some suggested combinations. Experiment until you discover the right marriages, as you did with other foods!

CHEESES	WINES
HARD *Cheddar, Gruyere, Ementhal, Provolone*	*Pinot Noir, Merlot, Chateauneuf du Pape, Chianti*
MEDIUM HARD *Monterey Jack, Jarlsberg, Colby, Port Salut*	*Beaujolais, Port, Gamay, Pinot Chardonnay, Dry Sherry*
BLUE *Roquefort, Gorgonzola, Stilton, Danish Blue*	*Burgundy, Port, Dry and Golden Sherry*
BLAND *Muenster, Edam, Samso, Bombel, Tilsit*	*Cabernet Sauvignon, Beaujolais, Pinot Chardonnay, Sherries, Port*
CREAM *Brie, Camambert, Bel Paese, Pont L'Eveque, Fontina*	*Chardonnay, Chablis, Johannisberg, Riesling, Grey Reisling, Semillon, Sauvignon Blanc*
FRESH CREAM *Feta, Boursen, Cottage, Mozzarella*	*Sauterne, Liebraumilch, Chenin Blanc, Gewurztraminer*
PUNGENT *Limburger, Liederkranz, Bierkase, Reblochon*	*Port, Sherries, Barbera, Gamay Noir*

FORD'S FIVE MINUTE

The Five Primary Steps to SENSIBLE Tasting

1. FIRST WE SEE
Everything about us contributes to our **appreciation** of the things we eat and drink — both positively and negatively. With wines and foods, the setting, those with us (or against us) . . . a wine rack, elegant stemware . . . a favorite wine label or the flourish of a wine steward . . . disparate influences combine to set **our bodily juices flowing!**

2. THEN WE HEAR
The clink of glasses . . . the gentle squeek of a corkscrew penetrating the cork . . . a murmur of guests about past wines . . . the soft pop of the table wine cork or the muffled explosion of the champagne at release . . . the first gushing flow to the taster's glass . . . the casual touch of bottle to rim . . . all buttress the anticipation of the initial taste.

3. THE NOSE KNOWS!
Hundreds of odors are perceived, recognized and catalogued **hourly** by the human's most sensitive organ — the nose. With foods, we effortlessly determine both acceptability and quality **before** we taste . . . flavors originate in the nose and finish on the palate! Because of its unique aging properties, wine possesses the widest range of odors of any food we consume . . . adding immeasurably to the **taste** and the **flavor** of the fluid itself and the foods it accompanies.

4. A TOUCH OF ELEGANCE
As the first hesitant drops of wine touch lips and tongue, a galaxy of simultaneous sensations clamor for recognition . . . the temperature first, and immediately the weight or body of the fluid . . . its texture and tenacity, rough or smooth . . . the thousands of papillae over and under the tongue sort out stimuli we know as sweet, sour or bitter (no salt exists in wine) in an infinity of combinations. Then we **remember**. We **recall** . . . other wines, other times and we **evaluate** and **judge**.

5. AFTERTASTES AND AFTERSMELLS
Not yet satisfied with the animalistic appreciation of the wine, man employs yet another level of judgement based upon a **finishing** process called aftertaste. In the process of swallowing, traces of the fluid often cling to the long palate and the throat — known as a long, or lingering finish, and an entirely **new** explosion of odors is forced upward into the nasal cavity forming yet **another** sharp smell of now warmed molecules . . . aftertaste is aftersmell!

THE ORGANOLEPTIC MACHINE

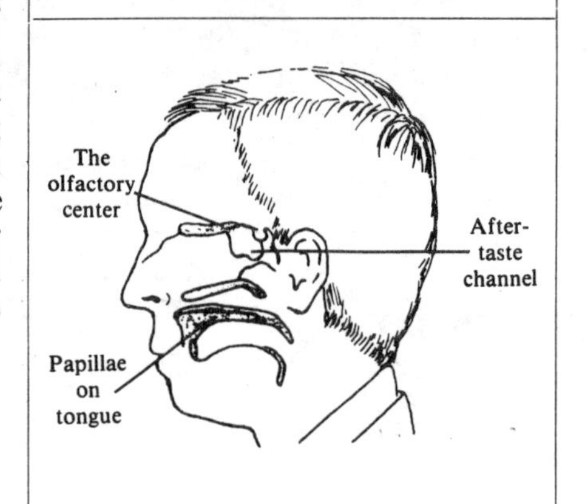

SOME ORGANOLEPTIC CONSIDERATIONS:

IN THE EYE — APPEARANCE

POSITIVE CHARACTERISTICS
Bright, clear, clean, full-bodied, color typical for type.

NEGATIVE CHARACTERISTICS
Cloudy, hazy, dull, sediment, color slightly off, crystalline deposits, body too thin.

IN THE NOSE — AROMA AND BOUQUET

POSITIVE CHARACTERISTICS
Distinct varietal characteristic, fresh, fragrant, fruity, spicy, clean, complex, pleasant, aromatic.

NEGATIVE CHARACTERISTICS
Distinctly off, moldy, green, over oaked, metallic, oxidized, vinegary, sulphurous, rotten eggs odor.

ON THE PALATE — TASTE AND FINISH

POSITIVE CHARACTERISTICS
Smoothly balanced, rounded, full-bodied, definite flavor, lasting finish, elegant, crisp, pleasant, sound, true to type.

NEGATIVE CHARACTERISTICS
Flabby, insipid, cloying, stemmy, harsh, bitter, thin, rough, flat, sharp, unbalanced, hot on tongue, unpleasant.

GENERALIZED TASTING LOCATIONS

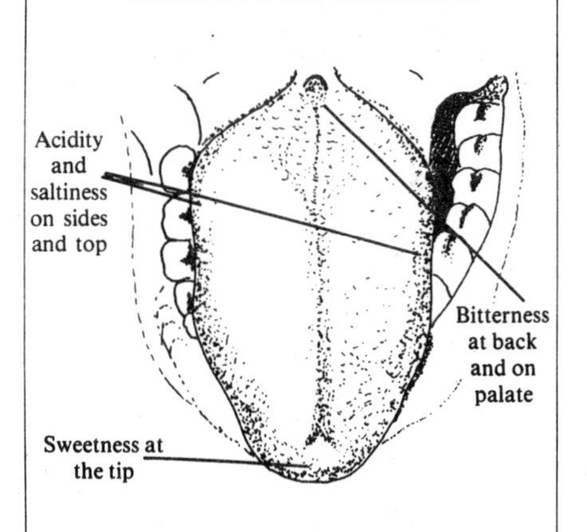

ORGANOLEPTIC ORGANIZER ©

REACTIONS

Eye
Nose
Mouth
Body
Sweet
Sour
Bitter

REACTIONS

Eye
Nose
Mouth
Body
Sweet
Sour
Bitter

REACTIONS

Eye
Nose
Mouth
Body
Sweet
Sour
Bitter

REACTIONS

Eye
Nose
Mouth
Body
Sweet
Sour
Bitter

How to Tend Bar While Smiling and Talking

Bartending is an art not easily acquired. However, the elegant service lies within the reach of all. With the proper equipment, here are a few professional rules of the roost for home parties.

Gene Ford

1. Limit the selection of exotic mixed drinks and prepare carefully all the ingredients and equipment in advance of the party. The style of the party or the time of the year will dictate the selection — Daiquiris, Cuba Libras in August instead of Hot Buttered Brandy and wine mulls. Of course, the standard highball and juiced selections should be available no matter the occasion.

2. Always measure your drinks — exactly according to the recipe book. Your guests appreciate the balance and style of favorite libations. Over-pouring or sloppy measurements are sure ruination.

3. Go first class and use fresh fruit and squeezed juices, as well as the best sodas and mixers. The best in booze can be lost in tasteless mixers. Fruit garnishes should be cut thick, up to a quarter of an inch so they don't curl in the glass. Twist rinds must be cut clean of the white matter. Be certain to wipe the entire rim of the glass before TWISTING to release a drop or two of oil over the surface of the finished drink. Oil cuts the hotness of the alcohol, mellowing the drink.

4. For sweetened cocktails such as the Old Fashioned, avoid confectioners sugar. It contains cornstarch that will cloud the drink. Simple syrup is best and easily made. If granulated sugar is chosen, dissolve the sugar first in a splash of soda before the other ingredients are blended.

5. Stir gently and in a circular motion. Agitation aerates and flattens the beverage, particularly if carbonated.

6. By contrast, when shaking, give it all you've got! Egg, milk, liqueurs and the like require violent action to emulsify into the creamy, foamy delights that satisfy both eye and palate.

7. Chill cocktail glassware — an hour or so in the refrigerator or five minutes in the freezer. It improves the looks, and the tastes. For hot drinks, place a spoon in the glass and pour in boiling water for a minute or so. What an improvement!

8 Use fresh ice, and remember ice will pick up odors from accompanying foods in the freezer. A quick cold bath will freshen it. Cracked or frappe ice can be made in kitchen food mixer, or hammered into shape inside a towel.

9. Remember the common measurements called for in cocktail mixes and stick to them: jigger — 1½ ounces; pony — 1 ounce; dash — 1/16 teaspoon; wineglass — 4 ounces; tablespoon — ½ ounce; cup — 8 ounces.

Of course, practice a few times with the unusual concoctions to gain facility in preparation. Finally, here are a few housekeeping tips. Place a toothpick through olives, onions and the like and use cherries with stems. Much easier to remove and consume that way. Rub the lips of pouring bottles with wax paper and the drops will disappear. Figure about twenty individual drinks per full liquor bottle. Add carbonated beverages just before serving to preserve the bubbles.

For the rest, relax and enjoy yourself behind the bar. Your guests will follow suit!

All That's Needed in Glassware and Equipment

Limitations in storage space and the fragility of most glassware are realities of life. The average kitchen soon abounds in mismatched units. To solve these universal problems, a little imagination and a penchant for uniformity of style will suffice. First, do not succumb to the exotic unless your budget for restocking is unlimited. Purchase sturdy, clear glassware. It's easier to match and allows greater visual appreciation for the creamy liqueurs and the happy champagne bubbles. Second, avoid the scallops and cut-glass effects for both of the above reasons. Finally, select a limited number of glass types and preparation tools with universality of use in mind. My suggestions follow for the all purpose, easy to substitute home bar.

Tools of the Trade

While often neglected, a simple ice tongs is an ecological necessity to avoid dirty digits in the ice bucket. Choose that ice bucket to serve also as a wine cooler for whites and bubblies, and make sure it has a lid to slow the ice melting. A nice, but not really necessary, touch is provided by a standard lemon-lime squeezer and it's flashy to use. Of course, the basic 1 ounce (50 milliliter) shot glass is required with the one ounce pour line. An abundance of both good and useless corkscrews are available. We recommend the standard waiter's tool for every household or the new Ah So. They are easy to master and the narrow steel worm of the waiter style seldom destroys the fragile cork. For other implements utilize standard kitchen utensils to stir, cut and serve.

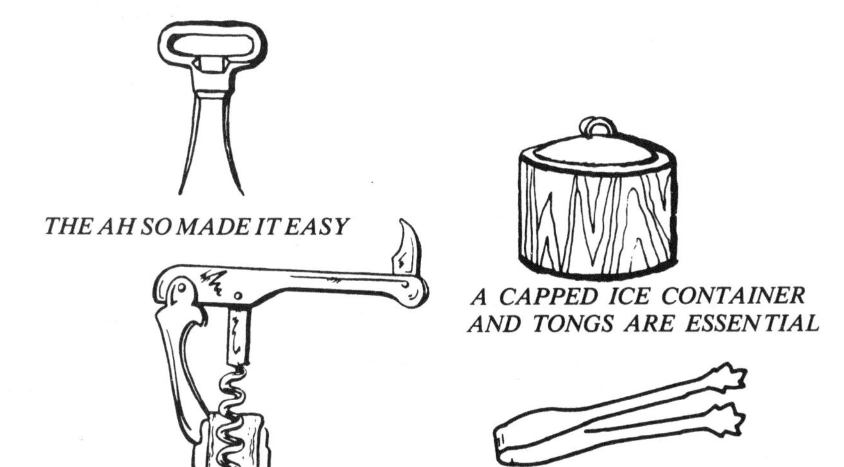

THE AH SO MADE IT EASY

A CAPPED ICE CONTAINER AND TONGS ARE ESSENTIAL

THE WAITER'S KEY A PROFESSIONAL AID

THE CLEAN AND EASY WAY TO SQUEEZE

MADE CERTAIN YOU POUR CORRECTLY FROM A PROPER JIGGER

Universal Glassware

The handy, dandy, and attractive ten to thirteen ounce Old Fashioned tumbler is the basic glass. For all specialty cocktails and 'on the rocks' orders, it suffices and it can also double as a fruit juicer for every day use. The nine or ten ounce highball or Collins glass comes next and is handy for flips and soft drink requests. A quiet elegance is mirrored in the one ounce, straight sided liqueur pony. You need only a half dozen or so and they accompany fine desserts with the perfect *elan.*

For the pre-prandial aperitif and the after dinner dessert wine, I suggest a slant sided sherry glass, but this luxury could be omitted in favor of the absolutely mandatory brandy snifter. Nothing can quite replace the delight of swirling that magical fluid in the bowl over the warming palm, releasing ethereal fumes.

In wine presentation, the trend is to the huge fifteen to eighteen ounce bowls on towering stems with the squat type for red and rose vintages and the taller type for the whites. For the practical household, the standard seven to ten ouncer will work as well, and can be utilized for whiskey sours, ports and sherries. For champagne, buy the tulip style to preserve the bubbles.

Finally, splurge on a half dozen pilsner shells for the brew drinkers. Nothing can beat the attractive and taste provoking two inch head of foam and the glasses serve many other soft drink and wine flip needs.

Drinking and Health

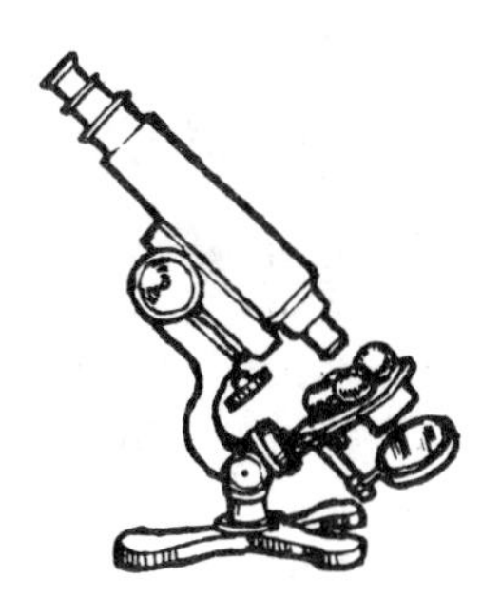

Alcohol is a substance that can kill you quickly and surely, but no more quickly or surely than water, if you drink too much of it at one time . . . in moderate amounts, it is not only harmless to the body but also beneficial in many cases.

Morris E.Chafetz, M.D.

Books like this one should not practice medicine. But, then, neither should government bureaucrats. Unfortunately, political objectives have been interposed in recent years between the public's right to know about drinking and health findings and the government's authority to protect citizens against themselves.

Over the last fifty years or so, there has developed a substantial body of science that finds real, tangible health benefits in drinking across a wide spectrum of human ailments. None of these data deny the awful and persistent costs of abusive drinking. Indeed an equally large and diverse science has aided the fields of prevention and recovery.

The problem lies in what the *Journal of the American Medical Association* called last year the physician's "conundrum." In the shrill, anti-drinking atmosphere engendered largely by federal health authorities, how can the practicing physician tell patients about these benefits without sowing confusion or being set up for future liability actions.

The simple reality is that ethanol, a natural by product of fermentation, is a key element in wines, brews and spirits. Without ethanol – as with coffee sans caffeine – our drinks would not enjoy nearly as much popularity. But the mere existence of a drug – in either beer or coffee – is not cause for the demonization that exists in the government's "alcohol and other drugs" linkage. This perversion denies to moderate drinkers – well over ninety percent of all drinkers – knowledge of the healthy properties of drinks.

Interested readers may want to learn more about neoprohibition (as in my latest book *The French Paradox & Drinking for Health*), but for the average reader it is enough to recognize the range and depth of drinking's benefits. Drinks have the following therapeutic properties: they tranquilize, reducing stress; they sedate, relieving fear and anxiety; they contain trace elements of all the minerals necessary for human life; they raise high-density lipoprotein, helping to reduce heart disease; they help catalyze vitamins and minerals in the diet; they reduce tension and restore zest for life in the elderly.

These pharmacological effects impact a wide range of illnesses, not just coronary disease. For instance, studies have defined positive impacts on diabetes, gallstones, the common cold, hepatitus, aging, stress, thrombosis and common tremors.

These positive aspects of drinking do not make ethanol a wonder drug. No one needs to drink to maintain a healthy lifestyle. Wines, beers and spirits are simply "other" good foods, when used correctly. But Americans do need better awareness of the benefits, as well as the dangers, to consume in a healthy manner. *Healthy drinking* should be the goal, not drinking for health. Fortunately government and public health hostility to drinking is yielding. The new federal dietary guidelines acknowledge some benefits in moderate drinking.

It's time for government and public health officials to drop the misleading drinks/drugs linkage. Our people can handle the truth.

Ford's Recommendations For Prudent Consumption

Don't be confused about your ability to hold liquor! Your ability to drive, to swim, to fire a gun or to perform any skilled and dangerous function is impaired to some degree by the consumption of ethyl alcohol in any form.

Alcohol relaxes the central nervous system and thereby slows reactions.

Authorities have clarified this condition in terms of your BAC — BLOOD ALCOHOL CONCENTRATION — literally the amount of the drug that is present within your bloodstream. A BAC level of a tenth of a percent is accepted most places as legal intoxication. At half that level — a BAC of .05% — inhibitions are lowered and judgment impaired. A one hundred pound person reaches *this dangerous level on the second drink!* As the concentration increases, stability decreases.

Study this chart carefully to determine your maximum consumption level.

A Guide to Calculate Your Blood Alcohol Concentration

(One Drink Equals a Shot of Liquor, a Beer or Glass of Wine)

Number of Drinks		1	2	3	4	5	6	7	8
Alcohol %	100 lbs	.029	.058	.088	.117	.146	.175	.204	.233
In Blood	140 lbs	.021	.042	.063	.083	.104	.125	.146	.166
At Various	180 lbs	.017	.033	.049	.065	.081	.097	.113	.130
Body	200 lbs	.015	.029	.044	.058	.073	.087	.102	.117
Weights					Physical Abilities Impaired For Driving or Other Functions			Legally Drunk Concentration	

Friends don't let friends drive drunk.

AWARE DESIGNATED DRIVER

Alcohol is "burned up" by your body at .015% per hour, as example, a 180 lb. person who consumes eight drinks in four hours has concentrated up to .130% of alcohol in the bloodstream and has oxidized only .060% leaving an impaired driving level of .070% in the bloodstream.

Wait until the body burns up the alcohol before driving or performing any life threatening function. There is NO fast way to sober up. Time is your only choice to prevent a disaster.

Then be conservative and reduce it even more as you are probably in a fatigued and excited condition when socially drinking! The calculations for the chart were developed at the Center for Alcohol Studies, Rutgers University. The chart has been widely distributed by law enforcement authorities.

Ford's Guide To Pronunciations of Common Words

ADVOKATT adh-vo-KHAT
Egg nog liqueur
ALAMBIC ah-LEM-bic
French pot still
AMONTILLADO ah-mon-tee-AH-do
Spanish dry sherry
ANISETTE ahn-i-SET
Licorice liqueur
ANJOU ahn-ZHEW
French white wine
APERITIF ah-pear-ih-TEEF
Before meal wine
AQUAVIT ah-kwa-VIT
Caraway flavored spirit
AUSLESE ows-LAY-zay
Wine from selected grapes
BARBERA bar-BEAR-uh
Dry red varietal
BEAUJOLAIS bo-zho-LAY
Light red varietal
BIKAVER beak-ah-VARE
Hungarian red "Bull's Blood"
BODEGA boh-DAY-ga
Spanish wine cellar
BORDEAUX bor-DOE
French wine district
BROUILLY brew-YEE
French beaujolais
BRUT brute
Dry champagne
CABERNET SAUVIGNON sew-veeh YAWN *Dry French red Claret*
CACAO ka-COW-oh
cocoa bean liqueur
CALVADOS COL-va-dose
French apple spirit
COMPARI com-PAR-ee
Italian aperitivo
CASSIS kah-SEECE
Currant liqueur
CHABLIS sha-BLEE
Dry white wine
CHAMBERTIN sham-bear-TAN
Dry white wine
CHAPTALISATION shaptilly-ZAY-shion
Addition of cane sugar to must
CHATEAUNEUF DU PAPE
sha-toe-NOOF-du-POP
French dry red Rhone wine
CHENIN BLANC shen-nin-BLANH
Medium dry white wine
CONGENGER KHAN-gen-er
Taste element in liquor

COTE d'OR coat-DOOR
French burgundy section
CRU crew
French vineyard growth
CYNAR CHE-nahr
Italian artichoke liqueur
DOUX dew
French for sweet
EAU DE VIE oh-duh-VEE
Water of life
FINO FEEN-oh
Spanish dry sherry
FRAPPE´fra-PAY
Liqueur over crushed ice
FRIZZANTE Friz-AHN-tea
Italian semi-sparkling
GAMAY gam-MAY
Light red varietal
GEWURZTRAMINER
geh-VERTS-trah-MEEN-er
Spicy German white
GRAVES grahv
Red wine varietal
HAUT MEDOC oh-meh-DOCK
Bordeaux wine district
LAMBRUSCOlamb-BROOS-co
Medium sweet Italian red
LIQUEUR li-CURE
Sweet spirit
LOIRE la-WHAR
French wine river
MARC mar
French for grape pressings
MARGAUX mar-GO
Bordeaux wine
MEURSAULT mehr-SOH
French chardonnay wine
MEZCAL mezz-CAHL
Common Mexican spirit
MIS-EN-BOUTEILLES
miz-ohn-boo-TAY-uh
French for estate bottles
MONTRACHET mohn-rah-SHAY
French burgundy
MOUSSEUX muss-SUE
French sparkling wine
MUSCAT muss-KOT
Popular dessert wine grape
NEBBIOLO neb-ee-OH-low
Italian red varietal
NOYAUX no-YOH
Almond flavored liqueur
ORDINAIRE ord-in-NAIRE
French for ordinary
ORVIETO ohr-vee-AYE-toe
Italian white wine

OUZO OOZE-oh
Anise liqueur
PAUILLAC po-YACK
Red bordeaux wine
PERNOD pear-KNOW
French anise spirit
PINOT NOIR pee-no-NWHAR
Red wine varietal
POMMARD po-MAR
French red burgundy
POUILLY FUISSE' poo-yee-FWEE-say
French white burgundy
POUILLY FUME' poo-yee-FUME-aye
French white Sauvignon Blanc
POUSSE-CAFE' poose-ka-FAY
Layered cordials
PULQUE puhl-KAY
Mexican cactus beer
QUINTA KEEN-tah
Portuguese vineyard
RETSINA rhet-SEEN-uh
Greek resin flavored wine
RHEINGAU rine-GOW
Germanwine district
RIESLING REES-ling
White wine varietal
RIOJA ree-OH-ha
Spanish wine district
SAINT-EMILION santa-ME-LEE-on
Bordeaux wine district
SAUMUR sew-MOOR
French white Loire wine
SAUTERNES so-TAIRN
Soft white wine
SCHNAPPS schnopps
Dry white spirit
SEMILLON seh-MEE-yohn
Soft white varietal
SOAVE so-AH-vay
Italian white wine
SOMMELIER sohm-may-YAH
Wine steward
SPATLESE SHPATE-lay-zah
German late picked grapes
VALPOLICELLA val-po-lih-CHEL-la
Italian red wine
VARIETAL vah-RYE-eh-tal
Specific variety of grapes
VINHO VERDE VEEN-vo-VAIRD
VOUVRAY voo-VRAY
French white Loire wine
CHATEAU d'YQUEM dee-KEM
French sweet white wine

ASK YOUR WINE MERCHANT FOR NEW SELECTIONS IN THE STYLE YOU LIKE

Ford's Garrulous Generalizations on Wine Buying

I will drink life to the lees

Alfred Lord Tennyson

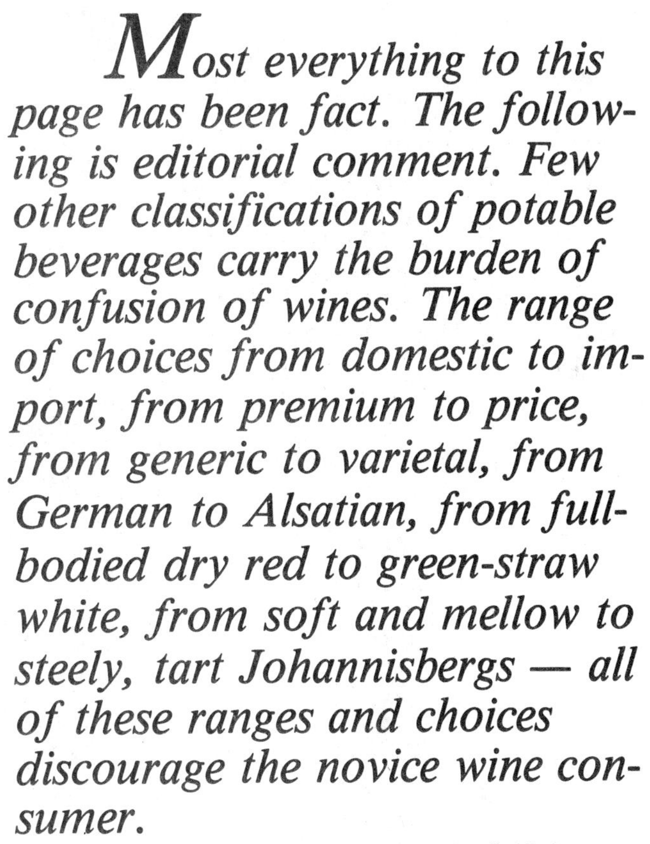

Most everything to this page has been fact. The following is editorial comment. Few other classifications of potable beverages carry the burden of confusion of wines. The range of choices from domestic to import, from premium to price, from generic to varietal, from German to Alsatian, from full-bodied dry red to green-straw white, from soft and mellow to steely, tart Johannisbergs — all of these ranges and choices discourage the novice wine consumer.

No other factor so inhibits wine consumption as the superabundance of types, styles and labels. Consider by contrast the housewife in search of beer or soda pop. If a favorite brand is out, many other substitutes will suffice for there is a general sameness about beer, soda and tomato juice. Remember, these are generalizations! From this broad perspective, brews, sodas and milks are more akin to each other than German and Alsatian vintages of the very same Riesling grapes, not to consider the ranges in tastes of the same wines from Monterey, Napa and San Juaquin counties in California.

Let's face it. The new consumer needs some easy handles and with the temerity of the foolhardy, here are mine that have helped during a decade of professional experimentation. First, semanticists agree that words describing foods mean different things to different people. If one person likes the style of a food or wine, he will use positive words, such as distinctive or assertive. Another judging the same item will advert to it as harsh and unpleasant. In wines, judge for *yourself* and recognize that you bring to the glass your own set of very personal, but very comfortable, prejudices. There are no absolutely right wines, though quite demonstrably there are some very bad ones. Since wines are foods, the beauty is in the eye, or in this case, the palate of the beholder.

Since wines are so diverse, chart some logical path and make a conscious effort to record the results of your experimental tastings — through all the wines of a company you seem to like; through all the same type of wines in your market; through domestic and imports in the same class; through price and premium. Don't get stuck in one jug. There are many pleasant surprises waiting for you out there.

Attend as many wine tasting parties as you can. But don't forget a little pad to record your reactions on the spot. You'll never remember the nuances later.

As price goes down, sugar goes up. Not universal, but the price wines appeal is to the natural sugar taste in America. Not a bad idea at all for the propagation of the industry in a country that consumes per capita in excess of 100 lbs. of sugar annually.

As price goes up, the style of winemaking more closely resembles traditional European. The Chenin Blanc resembles Saumur and Vouvray as Pinot Chardonnay resembles Montrachet. Premium wines are made from more costly grapes; are not pasteurized; and are aged to develop character. Price wines are, generally, from lesser grapes and pasteurized for stability. You get what you pay for in wines.

Most German imports, generics such as Liebfraumilch and Moselblumchen or varietals such as Riesling and Gewurztramier tend to the sweet side. Used often as aperitif or sipping wines in their homeland, they gratify the sweet teeth of Americans, and the Germans are very smart wine salesmen!

With the notable exceptions of specialty wines such as Cold Duck and Lambrusco, red wines tend to dryness. American vintners currently are experimenting with lighter, mellower reds — the Beaujolais, some Zinfandel and the Rose' of Cabernet and Pinot

MACHINES MAY IMPROVE THE MOVEMENT BUT THE WINE KEEPS ITS SECRETS *(Italian Wine Information Bureau)*

Noir. Search out these lighter reds as logical transitions from exclusive white consumption.

Americans talk dry and drink sweet. The amount of residual sugar has no intrinsic relationship to quality, only style. Ancient wines contained large amounts of natural sugar. Europeans love their sweet table and dessert wines. Don't be embarrased about your level of appreciation in wine. You wouldn't be about sugar in your coffee or the marzipan for dessert.

Pay no heed to the wine snob's derogation of dessert and aromatized varieties. Recovering from the 'wino' image, port, sherry, the vermouths and many other delightful sipping specialties are emerging as appropriate accompaniments to desserts and light foods.

Finally, as the Romans were wont to say — *desgustibus non est disputandum* — there is no disputing of taste. Whatever your personal proclivity, there's a wine out there to match it.

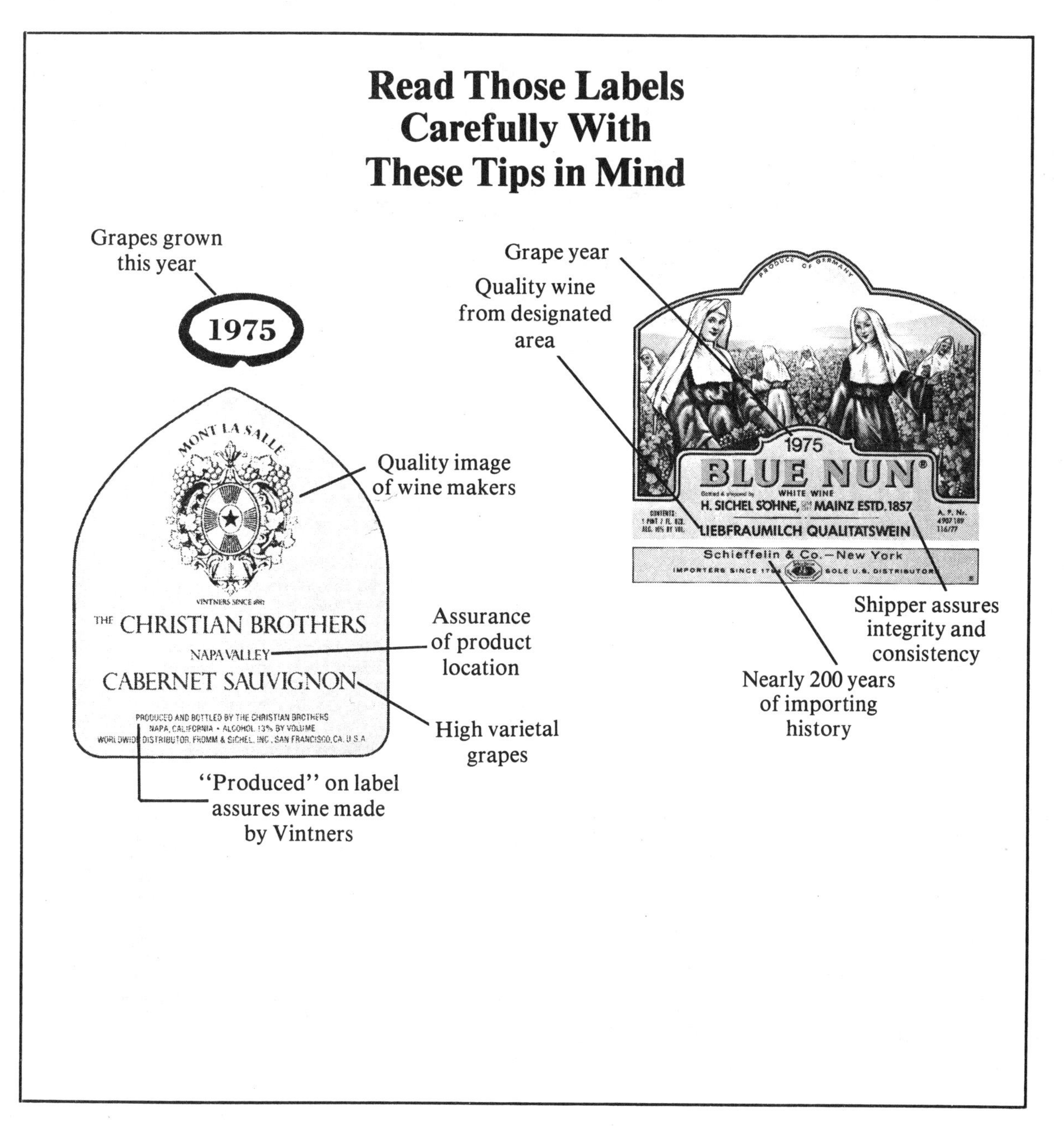

Some Excellent References

A Taste for Beer
Stephen Beaumont
Storey Publishing, 1995

Beer Companion
Michael Jackson
Running Press, 1993

Classic Spirits of The World
Gordon Brown
Running Press, 1995

Drink Moderately and Live Longer
Morris E. Chafetz, M.D. and
Marion D. Chafetz
Madison Books, 1995

Encyclopedia of Beer
Christine Rhodes, Editor
Henry Holt & Company, 1995

Evaluating Beer
Selected Contributors
Brewers Publications, 1993

Great Cooking With Beer
Jack Erickson
Red Brick Press, 1989

Preventing Alcohol Abuse
David J. Hanson
Praeger, 1995

Secret Life of Beer
Alan D. Eames
Storey Communications, Inc., 1995

Straight Up or On the Rocks
William Grimes
Simon & Schuster, 1993

Taste of Wine
Emille Peynaud
Wine Appreciation Guild, 1988

The Commensense Book of Wine
Leon Adams
Wine Appreciation Guild, 1991

The French Paradox & Beyond
W. Lewis Perdue and
Wells Shoemaker, M.D.
Renaissance Publishing, 1992

The French Paradox & Drinking for Health
Gene Ford
Wine Appreciation Guild, 1993

The Mediterranean Diet
Carol & Malcom McConnell
W.W. Norton & Co., 1987

The Malt Whisky File
John Lamond and Robin Tucek
Wine Appreciation Guild, 1995

The Oxford Companion To Wine
Jancis Robinson
Oxford University Press, 1994

The University Wine Course
Marian Baldy
Wine Appreciation Guild, 1993

The Vintner's Art
Hugh Johnson and
James Halliday
Simon & Schuster, 1992

The World Atlas of Wine
Hugh Johnson
Simon & Schuster, 1993

The World Book of Whiskey
Brian Murphy
Rand McNally, 1978

To Your Health
David N. Whitten, M.D. and
Martin R. Lipp, M.D.
Harper Collins, West, 1994

In Case You Wanted to Ask More

Wines

American Vintners Association
1850 K Street NW Suite 500
Washington, D.C. 20006-2296

California Wine Institute
425 Market Street
San Francisco, CA 94105

New York Wine & Grape Foundation
Elm and Liberty Streets
Penn Yan, NY 14527

Society of Wine Educators
132 Shaker Road
East Longmeadow, MA 01028

Washington Wine Institute
1932 First Avenue #510
Seattle, WA 98105

Wine Appreciation Guild
155 Connecticut Street
San Francisco, CA 94107

Brews

Institute for Brewing Studies
American Homebrewers Association
PO Box 1679
Boulder, CO 80306

Beer Drinkers of America
150 Paularino Avenue #190
Costa Mesa, CA 92626

Beer Institute
122 C Street NW
Washington, D.C. 20001

And Spirits

Association of Tequila Producers
World Trade Center Suite 147
P.O. Box 58083
Dallas, TX 75258

Distilled Spirits Council of the United States
12150 Eye Street NW
Washington, D.C. 20005

Rums of Puerto Rico
485 Lexington Avenue
New York, NY 10017

Look also now on the World Wide Web for many home pages on various drinks and marriages of drinks with foods. Many individual experts, companies, trade associations, and publishing firms maintain voluminous files and even complete publications and books on wines, brews and spirits on the Internet.

Alphabetic Index of Features